Days of Elijah

Matthew Partain

Bladensburg, MD

Days of Elijah
Published by
Inscript Books
a division of Dove Christian Publishers
P.O. Box 611
Bladensburg, MD 20710-0611
www.dovechristianpublishers.com

Published in the United States of America
25 24 23 22 21 20 1 2 3 4 5

Contents

INTRODUCTION

I heard the beating of helicopter rotor blades as they slashed violently through the air; at first, it was very subtle but then grew louder as the machine drew closer and closer. The sound instantly sent a cold chill down my body. The whooping sound the rotor blades generated was unmistakable. As I looked up into the beautiful clear Alabama sky, I saw the familiar red, white, and blue paint job on the Air Evac helicopter.

"Yep, that's the one," I thought. "That's the one Elijah rode in."

The pilot at the helm of the chopper banked the machine hard left. The sound ringing in my ears changed from the gentle whooping to an angry popping as he prepared to set it down in a green pasture that appeared all too familiar. I can only imagine how much fun the pilot was having with that maneuver. If it had been a few years earlier, I might have allowed that thought to linger in my mind a while longer, perhaps even allowed my imagination to take the place of that pilot and indulge in the dreams of my youth. But this was not a few years earlier; this was now, and before I knew it, tears were streaming down both of my cheeks. One glance at my wife, Paige, and I saw that she had the same reaction. We embraced right there on the spot, hot salty tears washing down to our now embraced shoulders. In that moment, unannounced to us, we were reminded of what might have been and the cold, stark reality that was. Something as arbitrary as the Air Evac helo landing in a field for our church's marksmanship challenge triggered emotions that took us back to a day when our lives were changed forever.

These are the moments that are the hardest, or at least it seems that way. These moments hit like a Mack truck and hurt just as bad. If you've ever lost someone close to you, then you know exactly what I'm talking about. On this beautiful and breezy March day, my family and I had come to support my daughter Maddie as she took part in a shooting competition, but during the midst of this seemingly ordinary day, we were blindsided once again by pain and grief. At times, it feels like those two emotions are never far behind me and will never stop their pursuit of my life. But in other moments, I feel guilty for wanting them to go away. I ask myself when this roller coaster will stop, but in truth, I'm afraid that if it does, I will have somehow forgotten how I got on it in the first place. Call me crazy, but I'm guessing that there are those of you who know exactly the feelings I'm talking about. If left unchecked, these feelings have the power to paralyze you. Sure, these moments are hard, but if I don't take the time to let them do their full work in me, then I have cut them short of their intended purpose. I must realize that God gave us these emotions, no matter how hard or cruel they may seem. They have the ability to do His bidding if I let them. But of course, I can also dwell on the physical aspect of them and drown in the sorrow they bring. The choice is mine. That same choice is yours as well.

With that said, I cannot continue until I tell you that this book is not so much about one particular day as it is an account of our lives over several years. It is a story of God's grace and His miraculous power. I hope that you will see the hand of God in it as I have and that you will be blessed in reading it as I have in living it. I also encourage you to take the time to look at your own life and see the ways in which God worked without you knowing it; how He has orchestrated His beautiful symphony in perfect time as you may have felt swallowed up by the chaos of the moment. For me, it is only in retrospect that I can truly appreciate the sovereignty of God. He knows what is going to happen during these times of trial, and instead of changing it to suit me, He uses it to push me into a place where the eyes of my heart are fixed on Him. I cannot think about it without being amazed. So many people on this earth, and yet He can operate with the precision of a surgeon in my simple life. How is that possible? Why would He even care? I guess the answer comes down to one word: Love. That's what this is, then. It's a love story. Not only the love of parents for their children but also the love of our heavenly Father for us. I can only pray that you see more than our small story while taking the time to read this. I hope you see with the greatest clarity that He is at work in your life as well with that same love, and it's that love that placed Him on the cross.

CHAPTER 1

THIS IS US

Jeremiah 29:11 (NIV)
"For I know the plans I have for you," declares
the Lord, "plans to prosper you and not to harm
you, plans to give you hope and a future."

Have you ever noticed that the telling of one story usually dictates the telling of another? That is the case here as well, because I cannot tell you about our son, Elijah, without telling you about us and our daughter, Maddie Grace. Our stories are woven together so tightly that you cannot fully understand one without the other. Her story sets up his, truly demonstrating the complexity of God's sovereignty, His awesome power, and His holy will.

So, before I get too far ahead of myself, I need to tell you a little bit about me and my beautiful wife, Paige. As of this writing, in November 2020, we've been married for a little over 21 years. She is, as she has always been, the love of my life. We met through a shipmate of mine, Allen Hayes, when serving our country in the Navy. More on that a little later.

I was born and raised in Pell City, Alabama. It was,

at the time, a small town 30 miles east of Birmingham. Today, it is much larger, and one might consider it a suburb of the Birmingham area. While the town I grew up in was still too large for you to know every person, you did know family names and where folks came from. My family name was often associated with cars, because most of the men in my family were mechanics and worked at Sutherlin Chevrolet.

Although we didn't live *in town*, our family home was located only a mile outside of it, across the Norfolk Southern railroad tracks, down Dry Creek Road. It is a small three-bedroom, one-bath brick home that my parents still live in today. We had the benefit of living in somewhat of a neighborhood, but also with large tracts of timber company land to explore across the dead-end road that ran in front of our home.

Growing up in Pell City afforded me and my brother, who is two years older than me, the opportunity to live as "country" as we wanted. Hot and humid summer days were spent exploring the creek that ran about a quarter-mile from our house. We caught crawdads, swam in it after a hard rain, and skated on its thin ice in the winter. Our only clothes in the summer were cut-off jeans; shoes weren't an option for us. It was all Momma could do to get us to wear shoes on Sunday to church.

If we weren't in the creek, we were outside throwing a baseball or running through the woods, exploring every inch that we could before dark each day. As the sun went down, we knew to come home before my mother began to yell for us. We didn't need a watch to tell the time. The setting sun was all we needed.

It was a good childhood, one that I am thankful for. Through their hard-working example and loving words, my parents taught my brother and me a strong work ethic and ensured that we knew the difference between right and wrong. We were held accountable for every action. There was no time-out or sitting in a corner for any disobedience. Any misbehavior was dealt with swiftly and justly.

My parents also made sure that we were in church. We were members of Arbor Baptist Church. My parents joined there in 1975 after seeing the church's ministry that followed a January tornado that ripped through town. They still go there to this day. The church is located on the eastern side of Pell City, in the old "mill village" side of town.

We were in church every time the doors were open, often being the ones who unlocked them. In my dad's opinion, if we were 15 minutes early, we were 15 minutes late. He has never been one to run late for anything, and our car was usually the first one parked outside the church on Sundays and Wednesdays.

My parents are both very hard workers. My father spent time at various jobs while I was growing up, but none of them ever paid much. Because of that, our family was always on a very tight budget, but we never knew it because our home was always rich in love. We never went hungry, and I'm not sure I ever walked out the door of my parent's home without hearing "I love you" spoken by both of them.

I have always felt my parents' love, and they have always been faithful to express it with words and action. It didn't matter what I chose to be involved in growing up; my parents were always there, supporting me and loving me with everything they had. They often did without just so that my brother and I could experience the joys of being a child. To this day, I am grateful for the sacrifices they made.

As you can imagine, this kind of childhood formed me into a man who knows the value of a hard day's work, as well as the blessing that a close-knit family provides. By the time I was fifteen, however, I had begun to somewhat rebel against my parent's teachings, and I strayed from the narrow road, so to speak. I'm sure I tested my parent's love for me in ways that I still can't comprehend, but to their credit, they modeled Jesus' example to me and always welcomed this prodigal back home.

My brother Jeff joined the Navy out of high school, so I knew that my path into adulthood lay along the trail he blazed, or at least one like it. He has always been more *book smart* than me, so if college wasn't in his future, I knew that it sure wasn't in mine. I'm sure I could have attended college, taking out loans or working my way through, but following my brother's example is always something I have striven to do. He has been somewhat of a mentor through life and has always been a voice of reason and caution in my ear.

I was a few months away from turning sixteen when he left for the Navy, and, to be honest, I gave up on trying too hard to excel at anything other than having a good time and working on cars. I had found a love and passion for mechanical things, and school seemed to hinder the life I wanted to live. Somehow, when I worked on cars, I felt connected to my Grandpaw Partain. It was like I could talk to him through the ratchets and wrenches in my hands. To see dirt and grease under my fingernails was to know him more, so I looked for any and every opportunity to put my hands to work so that my heart could be closer to him. He passed away when I was two, and unfortunately, I have no memory of him. So, I chose to create my own memories by trying to do the same work he did. More on that a little later.

After high school, I joined the Navy, just as my brother had done, and after boot camp and A-School, I was stationed in Norfolk, VA on the USS Saipan. That ship was an amphibious assault ship, but if you think of it as a helicopter carrier, you'll have a good idea of what it was. Onboard that ship, I met Allen Hayes from Leeds, Alabama, which is approximately nine miles west of Pell City.

Allen and I started riding home together every other weekend. To be honest, I was glad to share the time and expense of the 1500-mile round trip with someone else. We usually left on Friday once we were off work, getting to my parent's house in the early hours of Saturday morning. I would take him to Leeds to meet his fiancé after my mother had fixed us an all too early breakfast. We would meet up again Sunday afternoon after church to start our drive back, getting back to the ship most times after midnight.

I know what some of you may be thinking, *"You drove 11 hours one way to stay a little over a day, and then turned around and drove the same 11 hours back?"* Yes. Yes, we did. Any journey, no matter how difficult, is worth the effort if the destination fills your heart. My home, my family, indeed, everything about the wonderful area that formed me, recharged me in ways I am inadequate to put into words. Eleven hours was not too far, and if given a chance to say how far is too far, I'm not sure I could.

Allen and I came home for Memorial Day weekend in 1997, and I was looking forward to the long holiday weekend with my family. Allen had invited me to ride jet skis at his fiancé's family's lake home on Logan Martin Lake many times, but I finally agreed on this weekend. So, that Sunday afternoon, I found myself sitting at the dinner table with the Bailey family, about to eat grilled pork chops. Then, it happened. I saw her. And I mean HER.

Allen was engaged to Brandi Bailey. I met Brandi and her mother, Donna, a few times, but it was only long enough to drop Allen off on Saturday mornings or pick him up on Sunday afternoons. I had met Brandi's Dad, Randy, for the first time that day, and as we sat down to eat, someone new entered the dining area from a room in the back of the house.

I sat at the table, stunned. I didn't know who this young lady was, but throughout dinner, I couldn't keep my eyes off her. No, it wasn't what she was wearing, even though I can tell you that it was a T-shirt and cut-off jean shorts, but it was more about how she carried herself. I still can't put my finger on it, but something about her was different. Her beauty was unlike anything I had ever seen. She only said a few words during the meal, mostly just responding to someone else's inquiry, so I could not figure out her place in the family. I was hypnotized by this young woman, and I had to know more about her.

After dinner, Allen and I made our way outside to the deck off the back of the house. I immediately asked him who the young lady was, and I wanted to strangle him once he told me that her name was Paige and that she was Brandi's sister.

Allen lived on the ship in Norfolk, and I lived with a distant cousin in an apartment in town. Of course, no one wants to stay on the ship, so Allen would come over from time to time, often bringing along whomever he was hanging out with that evening. He also tried numerous times to set me up with a woman, although none of them was my type, if you know what I mean. Also, we rode home together every other week if we weren't out to sea. On those weekends, we spent at least 22 hours sitting side by side with nothing to do but talk and drive. And in all those trips, all of the times spent "hanging out," and in all of the hours spent together onboard the ship, there was never any mention that Brandi, his fiancé, had a sister. Hopefully, you can see why I was in angry disbelief.

Standing on the back deck, I asked Allan why he had not told me about Paige, and he explained to me that she had a boyfriend. That didn't matter to me, so, full of confidence, I told him that we would see about that. He chuckled and said through his laughter, "You don't know Paige."

A few minutes later, Allen and Brandi were ripping through the greenish water in front of the pier on the two jet skis. I was by myself in the porch swing that hangs on the back of the pier, and to my surprise, Paige walked up and sat down to hang her feet in the water off the front side of the pier, a few yards in front of me. My stomach tightened a little, and I gave thought to staying silent, but I had to hear her voice again. I couldn't waste an opportunity to talk to this young lady, so I cleared my throat, and words came out through the lump that had lodged itself there.

***

"They sure are having fun out there, aren't they?"

Paige slowly turned around, looked at me with a face that told me I didn't have a snowball's chance in Hades, and said very coldly, "Yeah."

My heart flipped a little as she turned back to watch her sister and Allen, but after another few moments, she got up, walked back to the house, and never looked in my direction again. I was smitten.

The next day, Allen and I made our way back to Norfolk after lunch. I'm sure the trip seemed longer to him because all I wanted to talk about, and know about, was Paige. I couldn't get the thought of her off my mind. Something inside of me was drawn to her, and it was a force that I couldn't resist even if I wanted to.

For the next month or so, Allen tried to avoid me. Every time I saw him, I wanted to see Paige's picture, and I wanted to talk about her with him. He finally asked me if I wanted to keep the picture instead of him having to go get it every time I saw him. I told him that would be weird, the thought of me carrying a photo of her around. I barely knew her. Then he said, "What do you think this is? This isn't normal."

Even those harsh words didn't deter me. He finally resorted to carrying the picture in his shirt pocket just in case he ran into me. Of course, he didn't know that I often went around the ship looking for him just so that

I could see her picture again.

June 29th, 1997, a Sunday, and I had duty on the ship. Allen was also in my duty section, so he couldn't escape my crazed and incessant stalking. But to my surprise, he came looking for me that evening with a sly grin on his face.

He told me that Paige and her boyfriend Justin had broken up that night after Justin had come home from a youth trip with his church. Allen didn't know all the details, but Brandi had told him that Paige and her mother were in her room, both upset, with Donna trying to console Paige. I immediately told him that we had to call them right then, returning his crazy smile with one of my own. I was going home the next weekend for the fourth of July, and I wanted to ask her out on a date. He told me that it was too soon for that, and I looked at him like he had a horn growing out of his head. Finally, after realizing that I would not be swayed against it, he called Brandi. She went into Paige's room to ask her if she would consider going out with me the following weekend, a guy she had only spoken one sarcastic word to.

Allen and I waited by the phone, my heart about to explode out of my chest. Finally, after what seemed an eternity, Brandi came back onto the phone and said that Paige would go with me to see the fireworks in Birmingham as long as Brandi could go with us. I didn't care if she wanted her parents to go with us; just being with her was enough for me.

My feet didn't touch the steel deck plates of the ship for the next week. I was ecstatic. I finally, *finally*, had a date with a *lady*. This wasn't just some regular woman. This was a lady, and I knew that a lady like that had standards that were way above someone like me. That thought scared me, but I tried to rest in the knowledge that God Himself had set this up.

I had taken a few days leave for the Fourth, so Allen did not come home with me for that week. The long 11-hour trip was spent going over everything I might say to Paige and how I would respond when she spoke to me. In my mind, I went through every scenario that might happen. I thought about what I would say, how I could gauge her reactions, but most of all, I knew I needed to be the gentleman I knew I could be. In short, Paige and I hadn't even gone on our first date yet, and God was already using her to mold me into a better man.

I was nervous that evening as the time grew near for me to meet Paige and Brandi in the Pell City High School parking lot. I changed clothes several times, finally deciding on the first outfit I had picked out. Running out of time, I got into my car and drove the short mile to the school, the tides of emotion rolling like waves in my stomach.

Paige and Brandi pulled up in her mother's maroon Ford Explorer. I got into the back seat, my nerves still a mess and my heart aflutter. Brandi drove, Paige stayed up front in the passenger's seat as we made our way to downtown Birmingham, finding a spot near UAB to watch the fireworks shoot off Red Mountain.

Paige and Brandi came prepared with a blanket to sit on, so I purposely sat down off to the side of it onto the hard asphalt to see if Paige would ask me to move onto the blanket, closer to her. Just as I had hoped, she called my name and told me that I could sit on the blanket next to her as she patted the blanket with her left hand. I knew it then. I knew it with everything in me. I was sitting beside my wife, if she would have me. I had never been as certain about anything in my life, but I knew, somehow, somewhere, deep inside of me, that this young lady was meant for me, and I for her. This was God's doing, plain and simple.

That night, after the fireworks, they took me back to my car, and before getting out of the vehicle, I asked Paige if she would consider going out with me again the next night. She said yes, and as I watched them pull out of the lot, I knew I was watching my future drive away.

Moments later, I walked through my parent's door, and my mom's first question was how the date went. I looked her in the eye and told her, "I'm going to marry that woman, if she'll have me."

The look on my mother's face was one of cautious uncertainty as she asked me how I knew that. I responded that I was as certain of it as I was that her shirt was red. After that, my mother left well enough alone and then asked when she and my father could meet her. I told her that I hoped before the week was out. My heart and emotions were a mess, and I couldn't think very far past the wonderful evening I had just experienced.

The next night, Paige and I went out to eat and then to see the movie, *Con Air*. Afterward, I invited her to eat at my parent's house, and she agreed to what amounted to a third date in as many days. I was working on another scheme in my mind, so that I could be sure this Justin guy, who was stupid enough to let her go, wouldn't be coming back into the picture.

The next night I wore my high school class ring,

which I hadn't worn in years. I thought that Paige would notice it, and if she asked about it, I had planned to hand it to her to see what she would do. If she simply looked at it, held it in her hand, and then gave it back to me, I would know that she wasn't thinking about us as a couple yet. But, if she put it on her finger, that was a different story. I would then tell her to just keep it and wear it, the implications of which didn't have to be explained. We would be boyfriend/girlfriend, a couple, and this Justin character would have no chance with her again. Shortly after picking her up, sure enough, she noticed my ring and asked if she could see it.

I took my ring off, everything going according to my crazy plan, and handed it to her. I watched her out of the corner of my eye, trying my best not to run off the road. Taking it in her hands, she looked closely at it, turned it from side to side, and then asked a few questions about my birthstone and the designs on the sides of it. The butterflies began to take flight inside my stomach, and then, I saw her slide it onto one of her fingers. I think my heart stopped. I really think I died for just a moment in that car.

A few seconds later, she slipped it off and tried to hand it back to me. I told her that she could keep it if she wanted to, trying my best to play it cool because I didn't wear it that much anyway. I added that being in the Navy, I couldn't wear it often, and it just sat around. She slipped it back onto her finger, twisted it a little, and asked if I was sure. "Of course."

With a smile reaching from ear to ear, I watched her play with it, the ring way too big for her delicate hands. She said she would have to get a guard for it and asked if that was ok. I told her it was and said, "It's yours now. You can do whatever you want with it."

For some reason, I still didn't have the peace I thought I would. Surely, she knew what this meant. But did she? How could I be certain? These sorts of things could be different at Chelsea High School. This might not mean to her what it meant to me. I had to be sure. My mind was running a hundred miles an hour, and even if I looked like an idiot, I had to be certain that she knew what this meant. That was a chance I had to take. After all, an idiot at rest is better than a wise man who can't find it. So, as we turned onto Dry Creek Road, I said, "I guess this means we're boyfriend and girlfriend?"

"Good Lord, I'm an idiot," I thought. I'm 21 years old, and she is 18, about to be a senior in high school, and I'm talking like a first-grader who just passed a note across the class. I might as well have said, "I love you; do you love me? Check yes or no."

To my surprise, as I nervously looked over at the beautiful woman by my side, she smiled, and as my heart melted, she said, "I guess it does."

The rest is history, as they say. A few short months later, in November, I replaced my class ring with a diamond one that reserved our spot at the altar. God had provided everything I had prayed for and then some. My cup ran over into the dish and onto the floor. Indeed, it may as well have been a fountain of His goodness. To this day, some 23 years after that first date, my heart still skips a beat every time I hear her voice.

I got out of the Navy on April 1st, 1998, and after a brief time working at Sprint monitoring cell towers,

I went to work with Paige's dad. He was an electrician and owned his own company, Bailey Electric. This job allowed me to earn money as I waited to be hired on with Alltel, a telecommunications company in Leeds. I started at Alltel in March of 1999, bought a small house in June, and Paige and I were married inside of Arbor Baptist, on July 24, 1999. Everything felt right, and life was good. We joined First Baptist Leeds, began a life together, striving to honor God.

In 2002, I took a job in Eclectic, Alabama, within the company I work for. This small town is 90 miles south of Leeds, and after selling our first home, we bought a fixer-upper log home in the Santuck community, a few miles from Eclectic. As our marriage began to grow deeper, we began to think about having children. That brings us to where this chapter started—Maddie Grace. The next chapter is the beginning of her story.

CHAPTER 2

LEAVING A LEGACY

Proverbs 13:22 (NIV)
"A good person leaves an inheritance for their
children's children."

Maddie's story began in May of 2004 when Paige and I found that we were finally expecting a baby after several years of trying, hoping, and praying. Those couple of years were laden with pages of ovulation charts, several fertility drugs, and countless doctor visits. The process of getting pregnant seemed so fast and easy for others, but for us, it was terribly slow and difficult. I have often wondered why so many people who don't want kids find it so easy to have them. And why do people who want them so badly struggle to ever get pregnant? I guess Paige and I should have expected it. Both sets of our parents had trouble having children.

My parents were told they would never conceive children of their own, but God blessed them with my brother and me. They had begun the adoption process but gave it up after my grand entrance into this world. Paige's parents struggled through several miscarriages before Paige's older sister, Brandi, was born, and like my parents, they were considering adoption before having children of their own. That fact alone should tell you what you need to know about our families—there's a lot of love to give.

Once we knew for certain that Paige was pregnant, we shared our wonderful news with our families, which was met with all the joy and excitement one would expect for a first grandchild. But as for me, I was still waiting on THE ultrasound.

You know the ultrasound I'm talking about. It's when you find out if you're expecting a boy or a girl. I made it no secret that I wanted a boy. The reason behind that goes back to a time before I was even born; in fact, it had everything to do with my grandfather, my father, and an old picture from 1976, taken when I was almost two years old.

My Grandpaw Partain must have been the best man since Jesus to walk the face of the earth. He was kind and patient, a man who helped others in anyway he could and served the Lord with a glad heart. By all accounts, he was an honest man and looked up to by everyone who knew him. He was also a man's man.

He took up the blacksmith trade at some point early in life after his father passed unexpectedly but changed his profession to auto mechanics after being kicked by a horse when my dad and uncle were little, or at least that's the story I've been told. His nickname was Pony, no doubt a carryover from his blacksmithing days. He could make anything; wood, iron, or steel; it didn't matter. If he thought it up in his mind, he could make it with his hands. My dad and uncle have the evidence of his craftsmanship in the tools that he made and passed down to them upon his death in 1977 when

I was just two years old.

He worked at various car dealerships early on, but his longest tenure was at Sutherlin Chevrolet in our hometown of Pell City. There he worked side by side with my Uncle Robert and, at times, my dad until the day my grandpaw passed. On that terrible day, he left behind more than my grandma, two sons, and three grandsons. He left a huge legacy and a void in my life that has never been filled.

I have been told that I was *his* baby. I am the youngest of his three grandsons, and apparently, I was very special to him and he to me. My parents told me that if he was around, I would not eat unless placed in his lap. If he was standing, I was in his arms facing outward so that I would see where he was going. In short, we were best buddies; the bookends of the "Partain men," as my Aunt Sharon called us; we were inseparable.

The picture I mentioned earlier was taken less than a year before his death. It is the six of us "Partain men" sitting on a couch at my Aunt Sharon's house around Christmas. Grandpaw, Dad, and Uncle Robert were seated on the couch with my cousin Bobby seated in front of Uncle Robert, my brother Jeff on Dad's lap, and of course, me in Grandpaw's lap. I have stared at that grainy and glossy image for hours at a time. We all looked happy, everything right in our lives and enjoying each other's company. But I can't tell you much about the man whose lap I was sitting on. I longed to know him, be like him, and feel the love I saw on every face in that picture. I needed and wanted my grandfather.

Grandpaw had two sons, Dad and Uncle Robert. Although my father was two years older, my uncle was the first to get married; less than a year later, he and Aunt Sharon had my cousin, Bobby. My dad married my mother a few years later. She is Aunt Sharon's older sister. With a set of brothers marrying sisters, that made our two families very close. I have one brother, Jeff, who is two years older than me. So, Grandpaw's two sons had three sons of their own. No girls. By the summer of 2004, my cousin and brother had all the children they planned; they were all girls. Bobby had a stepdaughter, and my brother had two daughters. It may not have played on anyone else's mind, but I felt like it was up to me (like I could control it) to carry on the Partain name; this monumental ultrasound would prove if I were up to the test.

Thursday, July 22, 2004, it was another routine ultrasound for Paige. No one was with us that morning because we weren't expecting this one ultrasound to be *the* one. After the first few minutes of finding the baby and the position it was in, the young lady asked us if we wanted to know the sex of the baby. I asked if she could tell this early, and she responded that she thought she could. As Paige and I stared intently at the screen, the lady moved the wand across Paige's abdomen, searching for the best angle. Then, almost by accident, it happened! We were looking at the front of the baby when it rolled backward and spread its legs for all the world to see. It was almost as if it knew what we were wanting to see. There was no doubt; there couldn't be. On the screen in front of us was our first child, and it was, most definitely, a girl.

At that moment, a switch in my mind was tripped. I can't explain the feeling that racked my body, but it was something beyond disappointment and despair. It was like a deep sense of failure. I tried my best to hide it from Paige, but it was no use. She knew me too well, and she could tell that something in me wasn't right. To her credit, she never brought it up. She allowed God to use it, and she allowed me just enough rope to hang myself with.

Once we were done in the doctor's office and back in the car, I informed Paige that no part of this girl's nursery would be pink. I told her that I hated that color. To me, in my deranged state of quiet rage, pink would be the constant reminder of the failure I feared to be. I felt as if I had let Pony Partain himself down. Of course, nothing could be farther from the truth; however, in that moment, as well as for the foreseeable future, I was saddled with a deep sense of failure. And as any good Christian does, I hid it.

One of the things Paige and I agreed on several months before were the names for the baby growing inside of her. We bounced a few ideas back and forth before finally settling on the names Maddie Grace or Elijah Mason. So, we left the doctor's office that day knowing not only what but who was coming to join our little family.

The next few months rocked on with no surprises or worries, and Paige, for some reason, had agreed to my insane request to boycott the color pink. Instead, we painted Maddie's nursery a beautiful bright yellow and were in the process of buying up all the necessary furnishings by the time November rolled around. We still had plenty of time to finish putting everything together since Maddie wasn't due until January 6th;

so, we were in no real hurry. Paige and I were going about our lives as normal, thinking that we still had a couple of months before everything changed drastically. But God had something else in mind. It was Monday morning, November 1st, and the next 24 hours would begin a season in our lives that would test our faith like nothing before.

CHAPTER 3

MEET MADDIE GRACE

Psalm 127:3 (NIV)
"Children are a heritage from the Lord, offspring a
reward from him."

At 30 weeks gestation, Paige's pregnancy couldn't have been more normal, and that Monday morning, we were going about our normal weekday routine. Paige was still working at a doctor's office in the town of Tallassee, which was about 30 minutes away. She worked in the lab drawing blood and taking X-rays. It was a job that she enjoyed, and we also liked the extra money it provided. We didn't use any of her income to live on because we had planned on her becoming a stay-at-home mom when Maddie Grace was born. That was an agreement we had made before we were ever married. We had many of those "what-if" conversations while we were engaged, and I must admit that those talks saved us a lot of frustration as our marriage matured. Paige and I were on the same page, reading from the same book and looking to God as our future unfolded before our eyes.

Paige darted back into the downstairs half-bath, laughing as she went. Apparently, she was having a hard time controlling her bladder that morning, and it tickled us both to watch how this pregnancy was changing her body. It seemed like we found something new to be excited about every day.

We laid in bed one evening with a microphone to her belly, trying desperately to hear our little daughter's heart beating. After a few minutes of frustration, we finally heard the rapid whooshing sound we were listening for. On another night, we played music to our unborn daughter. We placed a speaker on Paige's abdomen and played several children's songs on the CD player, all the while dreaming of the day she would enter this world. Although some days still felt normal, both of us knew that the time was ticking down. We understood that her body was going to change even more and that at some point, it would be a challenge just for her to get around. Paige left the house that morning having a hard time of it, but I don't think either of us could have been happier.

Paige always called me on her lunch break. We would talk about our day and just "check-in" with each other. That day was a little different. Paige called me from inside her car because she was drying her pants with the air blowing from the vents. We both had a good laugh about it, and the thought of my extremely modest wife doing this kept me smiling the rest of the day.

But that smile was erased when Paige called me a few hours later. The girls at work had convinced her to have her "pee" tested just to make sure it wasn't amniotic fluid. After a few minutes, their concerns proved legitimate and confirmed that the fluid was not from her bladder. She called her doctor, and the nurse told her to go to the emergency room immediately. She called me, and while speeding towards the hospital, I called everyone who needed to know.

The muscles in my stomach tightened as I entered the hospital and ran up to the second floor, where I found Paige resting comfortably in a small holding room with numerous machines hooked up to monitor both her and our unborn daughter. I could hear the quick, steady rhythm of Maddie's heart and the occasional beep coming from the machine which monitored Paige. But what had drawn my curiosity was a machine at the end of her bed that resembled a seismograph used to measure earthquakes. It was small and compact and had a needle steadily scratching across a ribbon of paper. For the most part, it was steady, but every so often, it would move up or down a little. Once the nurse came in, I asked her about it. She informed me that this cool little instrument measured Paige's contractions, or lack of them, in this case. I asked her if the occasional bump on the paper was anything to worry about, but she assured me that we'd see that needle of ink jump off the paper before Maddie ever thought about entering this world. My curiosity satisfied, I settled into a chair next to the bed to talk with Paige and laugh about the situation we found ourselves in. It seemed that anything we did was abnormal, so why should having a baby be any different.

The next few hours were spent calling our family and getting our plans together for the next day or so. Our plans were easy and straightforward. I would stay with Paige until 10:00 that night and then go home before coming back the next morning before work to bring her anything she would need for her extended stay. One thing was certain, however; she was not leaving the hospital until Maddie was born. That one thought had me silly with excitement, even if the actual event may be a month or more away.

The hardest part of that evening was keeping Paige's mother, Donna, in Birmingham. She wanted to come as soon as I had called her that evening, but I had finally convinced her to stay after being reassured multiple times by the nurse that Maddie's grand entrance was weeks away at the earliest. As a matter of fact, that was the last conversation I had with the nurse before leaving Paige for the night. She assured me that we would know hours, if not days, in advance before Maddie was born. So, I left the hospital that evening with a strange excitement in my belly. I was like a little kid anticipating what was coming next, but I had no idea that what was coming looked nothing like the thoughts in my mind.

It was almost 11:00 that night before I settled into our bed at home. It was lonely, and I couldn't sleep. My mind was still busy processing the day's events and wondering about the future. I wondered what Maddie would look like and what being a father would mean for me. Sometime before midnight, I finally fell asleep, completely unaware of what Paige was experiencing down at the hospital.

Paige was also trying to rest that night, but she couldn't. Pressure on her abdomen kept her from any kind of peace until she finally called the nurse to come to her room. A little after midnight, after talking with Paige, the nurse assured her that she was not in labor, and her discomfort was anything other than a baby trying to come out. Paige insisted that she thought this was not normal and that Maddie was about to be born. But the nurse, full of years of experience, shrugged off Paige's concerns and left the room, having tried to reassure her one last time.

Almost instantly, Paige felt a pain unlike any other she had experienced before. The pain forced her to sit straight up in the bed, taking her very breath as it radiated through her body. After 10 seconds or so, the pain subsided, but she was left with a strange sensation in her private parts. She nervously reached under the bedding, down between her legs, and tried to make out what was causing this awkward sensation. As soon as her fingers reached it, she knew what it was; one of Maddie's feet, hanging out of the birth canal, moving back and forth. The situation no doubt felt as strange to our half-born daughter as it did to Paige. Terrified, Paige pushed the emergency call button for the nurse once again. Seconds later, the same confident nurse came in to see what Paige needed *this* time.

After Paige's broken voice explained the situation to her, the nurse lifted the crisp white sheets. As the color drained from her face, she sprinted out of the room to the nurse's station. The call for help went out over the hospital intercom, and within minutes the small holding room was filled with people until they spilled out into the hall. Nurses were everywhere, trying to figure out what to do, because the on-call doctor couldn't make it. He was in the middle of performing an emergency C-section and couldn't leave the operating room.

On any other night, this would have been a major problem, but not this night. This was one of those nights where we got to see a little glimpse of God's handiwork. Would you believe that the on-call doctor wasn't alone? His friend, an OB/GYN himself, kept him company that night at the hospital when the emergency C-section call came. Instead of going home, he had decided to stay with his friend and help. This friend would be the one to deliver Maddie Grace, the one who would save her life in those first critical moments. Once he arrived and pushed his way through the gaggle of nurses crowded around Paige, he assessed the dire situation. There was no time for an emergency C-section, and, left with only one option, he climbed up into the bed with Paige and began to pull on Maddie's tiny feet. Within minutes, as Paige pushed and he pulled, Maddie Grace Partain was born, feet first, into this world at 12:35 am.

As soon as the doctor had Maddie in his arms, the nurse beside him cut her umbilical cord. She was then handed off like a football to a couple of NICU nurses, who had just shown up outside the door. The two of them took Maddie Grace in their arms and sprinted down the hall to the NICU. Once inside, they did their best to keep her warm until they could get an incubator ready. My daughter's birth had caught everyone off guard, and no preparations had been made by anyone.

I was finally sleeping soundly, oblivious to the chaos going on just 30 minutes away. Suddenly, I was rattled awake by the phone ringing, and, looking at the clock, I answered it at 12:37. The nurse on the other end of the line didn't have the same confidence in her voice as she had a few hours earlier. She seemed scared, her words chosen carefully and spoken delicately. After she had broken the news to me, she assured me that Paige was fine and that I could come down at any time. There was no mention of Maddie Grace other than the nurses had her in the NICU and were doing all they could for her. After hanging up the phone, I sat on the side of the bed, still shaking the sleep from my body. Was this a dream? This couldn't be real, could it? As I stood up, the gravity of the situation took hold, and I ran around gathering up my clothes as well as the items that Paige had requested. Within minutes, I was in the car driving as fast as I could to see my wife and newborn daughter. I frantically called our families to tell them the news as I sped down the highway.

I arrived at the hospital in record time, having run every red light and stop sign and broken every posted speed limit. In truth, I had driven that car as fast as it would go. I didn't know if Maddie was alive or not, so I wanted to get there as soon as possible. By the time I skidded into a parking place in front of the hospital, I had already made all my phone calls. Paige's parents, my parents, and her sister were all headed our way. I was looking forward to seeing Paige's sister, Brandi, most of all.

Brandi is a NICU nurse at Children's Hospital in Birmingham. I knew that she would be able to filter out any of the nonsense I might be told if Maddie were still alive. I didn't know it then, but Brandi would become much more than an aunt to our children. In the first few hours of Maddie's life, she became a source of strength to us. She could look at Maddie, the results of any test, and give us the unbridled truth about her condition.

After sprinting up to the hospital's second floor and down the hall to Paige's room, I burst through the door, not knowing what to expect. As a weakened Paige told me all that had transpired, I sat there in amazement and anger, soaking up every detail she shared. I was angry at the nurse, although the situation was not her fault. She was simply relying on her years of experience and knowledge. She was just as surprised as we were. But at that moment, I felt as though I had missed everything, and it was her fault. That feeling didn't last long as she came back into the room and asked if we wanted to go see Maddie Grace in the NICU.

She was alive! That was all that I cared about, as we trekked down the hospital's corridors towards the NICU. Nothing else mattered to me at that moment, and as I pushed Paige's wheelchair through the NICU doors, my stomach muscles tightened once again. This was it. I was finally about to see my first child.

One of the kind NICU nurses instructed us on how to properly scrub up each time before entering. After a while, this would become old hat; for now, we were like any other new NICU parents, scrubbing our skin raw, not wanting to hurt our precious daughter with any of our bad germs. As we finished, another nurse guided us through the maze of incubators to a far corner at the other end of the unit. We would later learn that this was the "sick" side of the NICU and was the area they kept the most critical babies. This would be the first day of many before finally reaching the "well" side and then eventually being discharged.

As our steps drew closer and closer, my stomach became a torrent of nerves and pain. I had never been so scared. My life was changing with each step, and there was no going back. Finally, we reached

Maddie's bedside. She was in an open-top incubator; no portholes or plastic were holding us back like other closed incubators, but neither Paige nor I had the nerve to be the first to touch her. Sensing our reluctance, the nurse whispered that it was ok for us to touch her if we wanted. We wouldn't be hurting her by doing it; in fact, it would likely help with the bonding process.

As soon as she had spoken those words, Paige dove right in. As Maddie was lying on her stomach, Paige began caressing her back with a couple of her fingers. I was still in shock, looking at all the machines she was hooked to and the tubes running into her mouth and nose. Occasionally, she grunted or tried to cry; but for the most part, Maddie just lay there, likely just as exhausted from the trauma of her birth as Paige was.

After some time, I finally reached out my hand and placed it onto Maddie's tiny back. The width of my hand covered her entire back, from her shoulders to the top of her rear-end. She was unbelievably small in my eyes, almost like a doll you would find on the shelves of a store. But something else happened in that first touch. Something new and foreign burst from within me. My heart felt like it would explode as it pounded within my chest. This wasn't nervousness or fear anymore. It was love busting out of the ground in my heart, not unlike a tender shoot breaking through the dry compacted soil in a garden. At that moment, as I touched my daughter for the first time, one thing became clear to me. There was nothing I wouldn't do for this little scrap of humanity.

Maddie's official birth weight was 3 lbs. 6 oz. She was small but not as small as others in the NICU. I cautiously looked around the noisy room at the other babies I could see. Some were agitated; however, others were resting nicely. I thought of all the parents of those little ones. How were they getting through this? What did they rely on?

I mentioned the noise in the NICU, and if you've ever been in one, you know what I mean. It is not a quiet place. Machines everywhere are alarming, breathing machines pumping, and nurses talking and cutting up. I was shocked to hear just how loud this place is. The little ones don't seem to mind, and even the parents get used to it after a while.

A little over an hour later, our parents showed up, and that's when the fun really began. Donna was mad at me, thinking that I had somehow left her out of this on purpose. After I had explained what happened to her, she shifted her focus to finding the nurse that sent me home. That was soon disregarded, however, as her focus shifted to seeing her first grandchild. After calming everyone down, I took them down the hall to the NICU's one viewing window. It was not much of a window. Most of the time, they kept the blinds drawn; but this time, in the early morning hours, the blinds were open. Across the room, under bright lights, I spotted the star of our show. I stepped back and watched as each grandparent took turns peering through the small shoulder-high window. They looked like children peering through a storefront at the toys they wanted for Christmas. Each one, tears flowing freely, had an unexplainable smile across their face; and each asked the same question, "When can we go in?"

After an hour or so of watching them watch her, we left the NICU window so that Maddie and Paige could both get some rest. By this time, it was early morning, and a few of us were getting hungry and sleepy. As we left the hospital that morning, I wondered how to find the sleep my body desperately needed. I was worn out but too scared to find the much-needed rest. After stopping by a local Waffle House, all of us, except Paige, returned to our home to try and get some sleep.

Once getting home, we all found a soft spot to rest, and before I knew it, I was being awakened by my mother and told it was time to get up once again. Only a few hours had passed by, and as we left my house for the hospital, I wondered how long Maddie would have to stay. I leaned over to Paige's sister Brandi, who was sitting next to me in the truck, and asked her what she thought. She told me that babies born this early usually stayed until they would have been 36 to 40 weeks gestation, but that it depended much more on the medical problems she would have. I swallowed hard when she spoke the word "would."

That one word opened a flood gate of worries for me. I had no way of knowing it then, but that moment was the starting point of a much larger struggle to trust God. Would I trust Him to be all that He has promised? Would I allow Him the freedom to be the unexplainable God that's found in scripture? Only time would tell, but I wasn't feeling too good about it coming out of the gate.

CHAPTER 4

A NEW NORMAL

John 16:33 (NIV)
"I have told you these things, so that in me you
may have peace. In this world you will have
trouble. But take heart! I have overcome the
world."

After a couple of days, Paige was allowed to come home from the hospital, and after everyone else went home, we began a new routine in our lives. Paige would go to the hospital every morning around 9:00 once the rush hour traffic was over with. She came home around 4:00 to cook supper, and after supper, we both went to the hospital to stay until 10:00. A few hours in the bed, and then repeat it all over again. On the weekends, our parents came down from the Birmingham area. Our fathers would help me finish the nursery while the grandmothers were at the hospital doting over Maddie. On Saturday afternoons, we would all return to the hospital to spend as much time as possible with our girl. On Sundays, after church, it was usually just Paige and I visiting Maddie. I liked Sundays. There was no hurry, and it was just the three of us. I imagined that this was what it would be like when she finally got to come home. I hoped it would be, anyways.

With that schedule, I didn't get to see doctors very often. They rounded in the mornings when Paige was there, so I had to rely on the information she gave me. Usually, after the doctor had finished with Maddie, she would call me and let me know what had been said. After Maddie was about ten days old, Paige called me in tears, sobbing almost uncontrollably. The doctor had told her that Maddie had a bleed in the ventricles of her brain. It was classified as a grade 4, which is as bad as they come. The doctor had laid out a prognosis that no parent wants to envision for their beloved child. I tried to be calm for Paige as she spoke, and I assured her that God would see us through it, although at that moment, I really didn't know how.

The seeds of worry that were planted a week or so earlier began to sprout that day as Paige spoke. I started to think about all the things I had no control over, and I began to give them as much credence as the reality I lived in. From that day and for the next few years, I would measure Maddie against all others her age, looking to see how her development progressed. That night, the nurses calmed our fears by explaining that we had not received a death sentence. Maddie was doing wonderful, and their exact words were, "Look at how the baby is doing, and don't worry about what the doctors say."

Within another few weeks, Maddie had been moved to the "well" side of the NICU, had begun to nurse from a bottle, and her brain bleed had been downgraded to a grade 3. Everything was going well, and after 6 weeks in the NICU, Maddie Grace finally came home on December

15th.

We had to spend a couple of nights in the hospital before they would release Maddie to us. This process was called "rooming in," and for once in my life, I was happy for the added caution. This was our first child, and I was nervous. I cannot explain the feelings that were going on inside of me, but it was a cocktail of fear, excitement, and foreboding. I didn't know if Paige and I were up to the task of taking care of this delicate gift from God. There would be no machine to tell us if her heart stopped beating and no nurse to assure us she was going to be fine.

After the two nights in the hospital, and with little to no sleep, we loaded Maddie into her car seat for her first ride home. The 30-minute drive to our home felt like an hour due to Maddie's screaming voice. She did not like her car seat, and she didn't mind telling us about it. I didn't understand how so much noise could come from something so small. For at least the next year of our lives, we would be serenaded by her screams anytime we traveled in the car. It didn't matter the length of the trip; one minute or several hours, she would scream the entire way. Needless to say, the longer trips were difficult.

Our first night in our home together was a joyful one. We bathed our tiny daughter in a blue plastic tub in our sink and quickly realized that she loved the water. From the first night forward, bath time was a good time. I took a few days off work to get settled in and into a new routine. *Routine.* Now that's a word that is foreign for the first few days and weeks when bringing a new baby home. *Survival* would be a better word. Looking back, it really wasn't all that difficult, but it was different for us as new parents. The long nights and tired days were just another welcome sacrifice for the blessing of the baby we had waited so long and prayed so hard for.

Over the next few months, Maddie continued to grow and blossom; in fact, by her first birthday, she was starting to catch up, somewhat, to other babies her age. She still was not walking, but she was progressing, nonetheless. On her first birthday, we found ourselves back in Dr. Fekete's office for her one-year checkup. We had a few questions about Maddie, but we were confident that she was doing well.

I cannot say enough good things about Dr. Fekete. She is the kind of doctor that feels more like a friend instead of a pediatrician. She takes her time with every patient and involves herself in the lives of those children as much as the parents allow. She is thorough, caring, and makes sure she answers every question you have.

One of our questions on Maddie's first-year checkup involved Maddie wetting her diaper every night. I guess I should tell you that this wasn't just a little liquid, but enough to fill the diaper and soil the sheet every night. Dr. Fekete collected a urine sample from Maddie and then sent us to the local hospital to have some blood work done. She was being cautious with Maddie, and as a parent, I was extremely grateful for her diligence. We returned from Baptist South Hospital a couple of hours later and were not at all prepared for what happened next.

Once arriving back at the doctor's office, we were taken back to a room immediately. Dr. Fekete explained that Maddie's bloodwork was abnormal and that she was spilling sugar into her urine. She asked if we wanted an ambulance to take Maddie to Children's Hospital in Birmingham or if we could agree to take her immediately there ourselves. *Wait! What?!* My mind could not process what my ears had just heard. Maddie looked fine. I wanted to ask Dr. Fekete more questions, but she insisted that there was no more time; we had to leave at that moment. The lab work pointed to Maddie having a severe diabetic condition that could threaten her life within the next 24 hours if left untreated. I didn't understand it but was thankful for a doctor that crossed every "T" and dotted every "I." If she was going to err, it would be on the side of caution.

We left the doctor's office confused, scared, and trying our best to get to Birmingham as fast as possible. It was normally a 90-minute drive, but we arrived at the hospital ER in record time. Dr. Fekete had called ahead, and we were taken back as soon as we walked through the door. Within minutes, they were drawing more blood and running more tests.

After a few hours, they admitted Maddie into the hospital in order to continue running tests on her. I was scared to death, and I couldn't understand why God would allow this to happen. Of course, this wouldn't be our last admission to a hospital with Maddie, but the first one really shook me up.

If you've ever been to a Children's Hospital, you'll understand a lot of what I'm about to tell you; however, if you've never been inside one, this may give you a glimpse of what it's really like. It's a very special place. It's where life and death collide headfirst into the innocent. Our family has spent more time than we ever thought possible within its walls, and I'm not sure there was ever a time when I wasn't moved emotionally as I traversed through the halls and passages.

Once inside, you'll see the smallest of the small, the sickest of the sick, and happiest of the happy. Yes, I said happy. I'll give you an example of that one. During this initial stay, I walked from Maddie's room on the fourth floor down into the main two-story lobby of the hospital. There are sofas and chairs there, a few tables, and a wall of massive windows overlooking the street just outside the building. I sat down on one of the sofas and began to question the reasons God had brought us down this path in our lives. The more I prayed to God, the more I felt sorry for Maddie and myself. Somehow, I had shifted into selfishness, and before long, I was only feeling sorry for myself, my thoughts nowhere near the God I claimed to be praying to. During that time, I heard a sound coming from one of the hallways that led into the lobby. I listened as the sound grew louder and louder until the source finally came around the corner into my field of vision. It was a small girl, likely 5 or 6 years old. She was walking slowly in front of her parents, who were pushing her IV and oxygen tank just behind her. She was pale, deathly pale, bald, and her eyes were somewhat dull and sunken. She held her head down, no doubt each step taking its toll on her weakened body, and she moved as if the next step could be her last. I wondered why she was not in a wheelchair, but that question was soon answered by the appearance of her mother pushing an empty one behind her. Her tiny frame was skeletal, and even though she wore loose pajamas, you could tell she was nothing more than a wisp of air.

I saw her and then immediately looked away. I had to catch my breath as well as the tears that had begun to burst from my eyes.

As she made her way around the lobby, I saw her say something to her dad. He bent down as she whispered in his ear; then, he picked her up to carry her in his arms. They walked over to the wall of windows, and I saw a smile move across her face as they walked closer and closer. They stood there for a few minutes, then I witnessed a transformation in her as they took in the early morning sunshine flowing through the panes of glass.

Her eyes lit up, and the once soft voice now squealed with delight as she could take in something more than the four walls in her hospital room. As they stood there, a transformation began within me as well. Who was I to be saddened by our situation? Before me was a girl fighting for her very life, and yet she was excited just to see the sun and feel its warmth. I felt ashamed. It wasn't the fact that this tiny girl appeared worse off than my own daughter but that she was happy despite her condition. She found joy amidst her struggle in the simple gifts of God. If only for a moment, she was a healthy and vibrant 5-year-old playing in the sun on a beautiful autumn day.

After almost a week in the hospital, it was determined that Maddie was as healthy as a horse. She did not have the problems they initially thought; in fact, the only reason we were there for that amount of time was because her liver enzyme levels were extremely high. Once they were near normal, we were discharged and allowed to go back to our everyday lives.

Maddie was hospitalized again the following summer for an MRSA infection, but we were admitted this time to Baptist South Hospital in Montgomery. It seemed that she had taken on her parent's unique ability to be sick with the strangest things. Even though we had a few scares, Maddie seemed to be doing well, and for my mind, that was a welcome break from the torture of worrying about the unknown. I wish I could tell you that I never once worried over my daughter's condition again and that I trusted God to be as faithful as He promises to be, but if you're a parent, you know that would be a lie.

CHAPTER 5

ELIJAH MASON

Philippians 4:6-7 (NIV)
"Do not be anxious about anything, but in
every situation, by prayer and petition, with
thanksgiving, present your requests to God.
And the peace of God, which transcends all
understanding, will guard your hearts and your
minds in Christ Jesus."

Once Maddie had turned a year old, we started thinking about another baby. Paige and I both wanted to have two children, and we wanted them fairly close together. What we didn't want, however, was a repeat of Maddie's birth; so, it was only after a consultation with her OB/GYN that we started trying for baby number two. He told us that he could not tell us exactly what had caused Maddie's early arrival, but as far as he could tell, nothing was preventing Paige from carrying a baby full term.

It didn't take too long for us to conceive the second time because just a few short months later, on Father's Day 2006, Paige surprised me with the perfect gift. I was taking my morning shower when I heard the bathroom door swing open. Next, I heard the shower curtain slide open behind me. Following that, Paige told me that if I wanted to see my Father's Day gift, I needed to turn around.

For the guys reading this, you can relate to what I'm going to say next. It didn't matter what I saw when I turned around because when a gift is set up like that, it's going to be good. As I turned around, my eyes were met with a positive pregnancy test and the news that we would be adding another member to our little family. I finished my shower that morning, dreaming once again of the Partain boy I hoped God would give us.

Later that day, as we celebrated Father's Day with our families at a restaurant in Birmingham, we told our parents by letting Maddie hold up a sign after lunch. It read, "I'm going to be a big sister." Of course, everyone was excited. After a trip to the doctor's office a week or so later, we found out that the due date was February 14th, 2007, Valentine's Day.

As before, Paige's pregnancy couldn't have been more normal; but to his credit, her doctor was extra cautious, so we were in his office a little more than we normally would have been. It was during one of these extra visits on Monday, October 2nd, that a routine ultrasound turned into THE ultrasound. Fortunately, our entire family was with us that day because we were leaving for Panama City Beach after Paige's appointment.

We were all huddled together, staring at the screen, and watching the movements of our unborn miracle, when all of a sudden, it turned around, as if to face the family it would soon come to know. Just as Maddie had done, it held its legs up, spread them wide, and almost immediately, every person in the room knew that our next child was going to be a boy.

I'm not sure my feet touched the ground for several weeks after that. We were having a boy! The Partain name would live on, and I would get to fulfill the dreams that only the father of a son knows. His name would be Elijah Mason Partain, and every night I went to sleep as he raced cars to victory lane, hit home runs for the Atlanta Braves, and ran in touchdowns for the Auburn Tigers. He was going to do all that he wanted in life, and I was going to make sure he had every chance I could afford to give him. All the emotions I felt when we were told that our first child was a girl were reversed. The excitement I felt could not be matched! The pride that I wore could not be equaled. I was going to be a father to a son! There was nothing that could bring me down from this mountain of joy!

I had prayed for this moment over and over every morning and evening. I prayed for the health of our unborn baby, that it would go full term, and that everything would go smoothly this time. I usually closed that prayer the same way every time. It went something like this:

> *"God, please let this baby be happy, healthy, and normal, and if I can ask one selfish request, let it be a boy."*

After that day, Paige's pregnancy continued to move along well. We were visiting the doctor's office every two weeks whether she needed to or not. I went to every appointment just as I did with her first pregnancy because I wanted to be present for every moment. By late October, Paige had begun to show a little, so we knew maternity clothes weren't far away.

We went to the doctor for another checkup on Monday, October 30th, 2006. After her usual ultrasound, the doctor came into the room. He told us that everything looked good, although I wasn't too comforted by the concerned look on his face. After a few minutes of going over the ultrasound, he let us in on the issues his face had already told us existed. Although the baby couldn't be healthier, there was a slight problem. Paige's cervix had started to shorten somewhat. Without getting into too much detail, I'll try to explain what that means.

The cervix is nothing more than the body's way of keeping the uterus closed. A mucus plug fills the normally open cervix. During pregnancy, the cervix stays closed until the last part of the third trimester. At that point, it "shortens" and allows the mucus plug to pass so that the baby can come out. In other words, a shortened cervix means we were at risk for premature labor and birth again. It was not the news we wanted to hear.

Paige's doctor, Dr. Griggs, explained that it had only shortened slightly and that normally he wouldn't worry about something this small. But with Paige's history, he was recommending that she take it easy for the next week until we could come back for him to measure it again. He called it "couch rest." She wasn't supposed to lift anything or exert herself in any way. She was to remain in the bed or on the couch. Now how are you supposed to do that with a little girl who is about to turn two?

I started making phone calls as soon as we left Dr.

Grigg's office, and before we got home, we had a plan in place. Our neighbors homeschooled their children, and their oldest, Kaitlyn Lightfoot, would come to help Paige with Maddie during the week while I was at work. She could do her schoolwork at other times, and her parents thought this would give her a good lesson in serving others. The next day, as I left for work, Kaitlyn walked down the hill to our house and started her ministry to Paige. That went on throughout the next week, and on Saturday, all our family came down as they usually did. Monday was going to be the only weekday this routine wasn't followed because the Lightfoot children went into Montgomery for school. I would take care of Paige that day and try to stay close to the house as I went about my regular workday routine.

That Monday morning, November 6, was just another day. I started the day at 5:30 as I usually do, and by 6:00 a.m. I was out running my usual three-mile distance in laps around our field. After I had finished, I came inside, showered, and got ready for work. After kissing Paige, I headed to work a little after 7:30. I checked my laptop as soon I got into the office, and I saw that I had been given a job in Camp Hill. I felt my blood pressure rise as I looked over the trouble comments in my job, because I really dislike going there, especially when I needed to stay close to the house.

Camp Hill is a dying town about 45 minutes away from Eclectic, the town I report to. To travel there, you must drive a winding two-lane road through mostly timberland, and if you're really unlucky, you can get stuck behind a log truck or two. That turns a 45-minute trip into an hour or more since there are few places to safely pass something that big.

I am responsible for three towns in all; Eclectic, Kowaliga, and Camp Hill. Eclectic is only 15 minutes from my house, so I could help Paige easily from there. Kowaliga is just a few miles up the road from Eclectic, but Camp Hill is the farthest and most aggravating of all of them. Camp Hill was being the usual thorn in my side that morning and making my life very difficult. That's the nature of my job, however, and since I am the only one who does it, I had no choice.

I left for Camp Hill shortly before 8:00. Once I got there, I isolated and repaired the trouble I was dispatched on fairly quickly. I looked at my watch, and to my surprise, it was only 8:55. Even though I really needed to get back towards Eclectic, I decided to take a detour from the usual way back and go down Highway 280 into Opelika.

We were in the process of remodeling our kitchen, and we were looking for some specific cabinet pulls at Target. We hadn't been able to find them anywhere else, and since I wasn't that far from Opelika, I decided to go there. It would only add 15 minutes to my trip back, and I rationalized it by thinking that I would more than likely be behind a log truck or two anyways. That would make the time driving back equal. Also, there isn't any cell phone coverage between Camp Hill and Eclectic, and I wanted to call Paige once I was sure she was up and about. So, I left the Camp Hill office and hurried towards the Target in Opelika.

It didn't take me long to get to Target and see that they did not have the cabinet pulls we were looking for. Disappointed, I got back into my truck and pulled out of the parking lot. Before I could get more than a hundred yards away, my phone started ringing. I looked down to see who was calling, hoping it wasn't work again, and I saw that it was Paige.

Butterflies. Yes, I still get butterflies in my stomach whenever my wife calls me or looks me in the eye. I'm not sure why it's that way, but it's a feeling that I hope never changes. I love my wife with everything I have, and I guess that feeling leaks out a little into my gut as I realize that she loves me the same.

I looked at the clock on the truck radio, and it was 9:27. I answered the phone expecting to hear my wife's sweet voice on the other end, but as soon as she spoke, I knew something was terribly wrong. The words that came out of her mouth sent a cold chill through my body that settled into a hard lump in my stomach. The butterflies were chased away by a cold and dark feeling that was all too familiar. My mind could not process it fast enough, and my heart sank into a bottomless pit as she spoke the words,

"Something is wrong; I'm having this baby."

I'm not sure you can ever prepare yourself for moments like the one Paige and I found ourselves in that morning. Her pregnancy was almost at 25 weeks, a good 3 months before the due date of February 14th. What do you say in a time like this? What can you say? What can you do? The only thing I could think to tell her was to call 911 and then to call someone else to come help. I hung up the phone, pushed the accelerator to the floor, and pointed my truck in the direction of I-85.

I sat angrily behind a lumber truck from Lowe's in the turn lane to get onto the interstate. He had 2x4's piled 5-feet-high on the bed, and I knew this ordeal was costing me precious moments. When the turn light turned green, he turned ever so slowly to get onto the on-ramp of the interstate. Suddenly, his load shifted, and the pile of 2x4's cascaded off the bed of his truck onto the right shoulder of the road. I sped past him on the left side of the on-ramp and floored the accelerator once again, tires squealing as I gained speed through the sharp double-back turn of the on-ramp. Once on the interstate, I quickly found out that the truck cut off at 118 mph, so I did my best to keep it at 115. I had my emergency flashers on, and I passed people wherever I could; the left, right, or on the shoulder of the road, I didn't care because I knew this was absolutely a matter of life and death.

During this NASCAR-style scene, I was steadily making phone calls. My first call was, oddly enough, to our church. I knew none of our neighbors were home, and I wanted to get someone to the house to help with Maddie Grace. One of the secretaries answered the phone, and I asked to speak to Brother Randy Godfrey, our Associate Pastor of Worship. He was not in yet, so I asked who was there. I was told that Brother Larry Gore was there. He is our Associate Pastor of Administration and Counseling. I asked to speak to him, and after a few seconds on hold, I heard his familiar voice on the other end of the line.

Somehow, despite the circumstances, I was completely calm. I asked Brother Larry if he knew where I lived, and after confirming that he did, I asked him if he could go by there for me. Once he said yes, I laid the news on him. Talk about setting someone up; I would love to know what went through his mind when I told him that Paige was having our very premature baby at home, and I was asking him to jump in the middle of this terrible situation. Oddly enough, he was calm as well. He said he would take care of it, and I hung up the phone, assured that Paige would not be alone for very long.

My other calls were to my work, and of course, to our families. I had no news to give them other than the seven words Paige had spoken to me, but that was enough to get our families headed our way and others praying for us before we even knew what to pray for. God knew what was going on, and even though I didn't realize it then, He was already at work in the midst of our terrible situation.

I made the trip from Opelika to our home in a little over 30 minutes. It's usually an hour's drive, but I had broken every law that pertains to the operation of a vehicle in the state of Alabama. I sped down our dirt road and driveway, and as I came down the hill in view of our house, my eyes were met with a scene from a movie. Sheriff's cars, ambulances, and volunteer firefighter's cars were everywhere. I had to slide my truck to a stop on the other side of the bridge that spans the creek in front of our home. I ran across the bridge, up the walkway, and sprinted up the stairs of our front porch, where I was met by Brother Larry. He had Maddie Grace in his arms and our phone in the front pocket of his button-down shirt. What I saw somehow gave me a little comfort. Brother Larry had told me on the phone that he would take care of it, and with what my eyes were seeing, he had done just what he said he would do.

Brother Larry asked me what I knew, and, through my quick, shallow breaths, I told him that I knew nothing but what Paige had told me. He then said to me that Paige had delivered the baby, that she was fine, and that the paramedics were working on our newborn son upstairs in our bedroom.

Something inside of me, something very primal, took over at that moment. I can't describe it other than to say that everything I am needed to get to Paige. I had to see her, comfort her, and let her know that I was there. Nothing else mattered to me until I could do those things. I didn't know what she had been through, but over the next few weeks, as the story God was writing came into focus, I would see that our family was in the middle of something very special. We were living out a miracle.

Once I had left for work that morning, Paige got up and went downstairs. She ate a small breakfast and sat on the couch until Maddie woke up and wanted out of her bed an hour or so later. She fixed Maddie a quick breakfast and returned to the couch where the two of them watched cartoons together. Suddenly, and without warning, she felt the pains of childbirth overtake her body, just as it had done in that small holding room two years earlier. Instantly scared, she staggered up the stairs to our bedroom, picked up the phone, and dialed my number.

After the two of us hung up, Paige went into our bathroom, leaving Maddie to climb the stairs by herself a few moments later. As Paige closed the door behind the two of them, she knew that she was out of time, and after collapsing down on the toilet, Elijah Mason Partain was born.

Paige caught him in her hands as he came out of her body, and she held his tiny frame in one hand as she dialed 911 with the other. She knew in her heart what this meant. After she had hung up the phone with the dispatcher, she and Maddie talked to Elijah and begged him to hold on until help could arrive.

The help that would come showed up first in two Deputy Sheriffs. Deputy Stan Hinson was the first on the scene, and after Paige would not come to the door, he began to yell for her from outside in the yard. During that time, another Deputy, Jason Chambers, arrived. Once they figured out where Paige was, they entered our home and went upstairs to assess the situation. A few minutes later, Brother Larry arrived from our church with one of the secretaries, Mrs. Beth Yates. She would be the one to cut Elijah's umbilical cord. Once inside, Brother Larry took charge of Maddie Grace and allowed the other three to tend to Paige and Elijah.

Fortunately, Deputy Jason Chambers' wife is an OB nurse, and as he was speeding towards our home that morning, she guided him through the process of cutting Elijah's umbilical cord and starting CPR on him. When the Montgomery Advertiser newspaper interviewed him about it a few days later, he stated that he would rather have gone into a house and confronted a man with a gun. He said he was trained to handle that situation and would have felt more comfortable, but handling a premature infant in this situation was something that no training can fully prepare someone for. Later, both he and Stan Hinson would earn an award as Deputies of the Year for their efforts that morning; however, in my mind, they earned something much more meaningful that day. I know they were "just doing their job," but the gift I was given by them can never be fully expressed.

Once the deputies had finished with all they could do, the paramedics finally arrived and started working to save Elijah in earnest. During this time, as I was driving like a crazed maniac, word was getting out to our church family, who came quickly to our side to support us.

There is no way I could remember to thank everyone who helped us that day and who gave of their time and energy to show us the face of God in one of our darkest hours. They were like angels, surrounding us with love and prayer and jumping in to meet every need we had. They enabled me to be a husband to Paige and continue to fulfill the vows I had spoken the day we wed. But that's what God calls us to do as the living body of His Son, isn't it? What we experienced that day was nothing more than the church being the church of the living God.

Once inside our home, I ran upstairs looking for Paige. I had been told by Brother Larry that she was in our bathroom and that it had served as our son's delivery room. I entered our bedroom and saw two paramedics surrounding a small object on our bed. They were working feverishly on what I assumed was our newborn son. I glanced that way, but I continued to follow the yearnings of my heart for Paige.

As I entered our small bathroom, I saw Paige sitting on the toilet with a paramedic attending to her. She was bent over, her head in her hands, and she was quietly sobbing. She looked up as I entered, and after kneeling down in front of her, we embraced. Through my own tears, I prayed a quiet prayer in her ear, and afterward, I whispered to her that this was not her fault. I don't know why I spoke those words, but something inside me knew that she would blame herself for the situation we found ourselves in. I told her that we would trust God with this baby as we had done before and that nothing was too big for Him.

After spending a few minutes with her, I walked out of the bathroom and into our bedroom, where the paramedics were working on our son. One of the two walked away as I approached, only briefly making eye contact with me before hanging his head, and the other stayed there beside Elijah and helped him to breathe in the oxygen they were administering. We did not speak to each other, but our eyes met, and I could tell from his gaze that this might be the only time I would see my son alive.

As I turned my eyes to my son, I realized that I was looking at the one I had prayed so long for, and, at that moment, it didn't even seem real. He was tiny, smaller than any baby doll I had ever seen. His skin was almost a purple color, and he gasped for air like a fish out of water. He wasn't moving much, and upon my initial assessment, I didn't give him much of a chance to make it.

The lone paramedic beside him finally spoke in a hushed voice. He told me that he had a good heartbeat and that the Air Evac helicopter was on its way. I silently hoped that he could make it that long, but considering what my eyes saw, I didn't think he could.

A few minutes later, I heard the sound of a helicopter in the distance. Almost immediately, the traffic and noise within our bedroom began to pick up. I had spent the few minutes that had passed going between Paige, Maddie, and Elijah. I didn't know where to be, not wanting to focus on one and leave the other two out. I stayed with Elijah whenever I knew the helicopter was close, and as people began to surround us, I finally heard one of the static-filled voices on the radio signal that it was time to go.

The paramedic who had stayed with Elijah picked him up, and another handled all the gear they had hooked to him. They walked very quickly down the stairs and outside the house into our yard.

The day was still cool, there was a strong southern wind blowing in, and there weren't any clouds to be seen. My senses were overloaded as we hastily walked towards the field I ran in just hours earlier. Fluorescent ribbon laid out by volunteer firemen marked off the landing area for the helicopter, and we paused for a moment in the yard as it landed a few hundred feet away. I didn't know how far I could go, so, through the noise, I asked the medic to let me know when to stop. He shook his head in agreement, and we continued towards the noisy aircraft.

A few moments later, the helicopter's flight nurse, John Fryer, jumped out of the helicopter and ran to meet us about 50 feet from it. The medic, cradling Elijah in his arms, began telling John exactly what they had done to keep my son alive thus far. John, taking my son in his arms, leaned in so that I could hear him above

the noise and asked me if I wanted to tell him goodbye.
I nodded my head and leaned into the blanket. I kissed
my son on his head, told him to be strong, and asked
John to take care of my son. He nodded his head in
affirmation, all of us struggling to hear over the noise of
the helicopter, and then he sped off, jumping inside the
helicopter with my son in his arms and the medic's gear
slung over his shoulder.

As I watched this unfold, I was sure I had seen
Elijah alive for the last time. A few moments later, the
engine of the helicopter began to rev up and whistle even
louder. The blades started to spin faster and chop the
air up in a fit of energy. Finally, the pilot of the aircraft
raised it up off the ground slowly. Once it was a good ten
feet off the ground, he started to spin counterclockwise
into the wind. As soon as he was above the trees, he
stopped for a moment. The helicopter swayed a little as
it caught the strong wind coming in over the trees, but
as soon as the machine settled back down, he poured
the fuel to it. The front of the helicopter dove down
towards the ground, and the rotors began to work even
harder to get the aircraft up to speed. You could hear
each individual blade crack its way through the air as
the aircraft fought for speed and altitude.

As I watched it leave, growing smaller in the distance,
the reality of the situation took hold. I could stand the
pressure no longer, and I broke down into a heap as
tears burst from my eyes. I sobbed uncontrollably and
could not stop. Someone from behind grabbed me and
started praying, and then without warning, I felt others
join in, a mass of broken humanity, in worship, pleading
the same cry of desperation to our heavenly Father.

I recognized the voice praying over me. It was Randy Godfrey, our Music Minister. I wondered when he had gotten there because I hadn't seen him drive up. Once he had finished praying, I looked up to see at least a dozen people surrounding us. Most of them were people from our church, but there were also volunteer firemen, and I did notice that one of the medics who had attended to Elijah had joined us as well. I turned around to walk towards the house so that I could see how Paige was doing, but my eyes were met by the sight of Brian and April Sexton. As soon as I saw them, I broke down again.

I first met the Sextons right after we had joined Santuck Baptist Church. One Sunday, shortly after, Paige and I were going to try to find a Sunday School class but had arrived at church late. We didn't feel very comfortable bursting into a class that had already started, especially since we did not know anyone yet. But as soon as we drove into the parking lot, we noticed a young lady around our age walking towards the church. We asked her if she knew the location of a class we could attend. She said she was going to the one she attended and was running late as well. As you may have figured, that young woman was April, and she led us to the class we would eventually become a part of.

After that day, we got to know the Sextons a little better, but I wouldn't have called us best friends. We were in the same class, had similar interests, and hung around some of the same people. We would eventually be part of the band, Elijah's Promise, for a few years with my neighbor, Darin Lightfoot. You may remember that it was his daughter, Kaitlyn, that was helping Paige with Maddie.

The Sexton's presence that day was a gift from God. You see, a few months earlier, on June 15th, they lost their oldest son, Austin, in a car wreck. April and their other son, Barrett, were severely injured, but Austin had died on the scene. I received a phone call from Darin Lightfoot that morning letting me know of the accident. Without knowing why, I went down to the hospital to be with Brian. Of course, the hallways surrounding the ER were packed with people, and I wasn't sure why God had prompted me to go to them. What could I do for them at that moment?

I stood in the overcrowded hallway as Brian emerged from the back of the ER. Our eyes met, and he came to me, through the others that were there, in tears. Our embrace lasted for a minute or longer, and I struggled with the words to say. What could I tell him? What words of comfort did I have? None. I had nothing. That was the first lesson I would learn in ministering to those who are hurting the most. Sometimes it's just being there that really counts. Brian pulled back from our embrace and asked me if I would like to go see April. How could I say no? I agreed, and he took me back into one of the scariest situations I have ever been in.

I saw April lying on a gurney in the middle of the ER with her mother sitting beside her. As I approached the two of them, my stomach became uneasy. I still had no words to say, and I didn't know what to do. April looked at me, and almost without warning, I leaned in, began to speak, and patted one of her shoulders with my hand. To this day, I cannot tell you what I said. I'm not sure if I comforted her or if I put my foot in my mouth.

Finally, April looked up to me and said, "Matt, I'm on a lot of pain medicine right now, so I'm not feeling much. But I can tell you that the shoulder you're patting is the one that's broken."

I couldn't have felt worse, but we both laughed out loud at my folly. Even today, April and I laugh about it, and I would like to think that I gave her a little levity in her darkest hour.

That day was Thursday, June 15th and just happened to be three days before Paige would tell me that she was pregnant with Elijah. For that reason, we did not tell anyone at church about it. We wanted to respect the Sextons and the memory of Austin. It just didn't seem right to share our joy with everyone while they were going through so much heartache.

I looked into Brian and April's eyes that November morning and they were both filled with tears. They knew. I didn't have to say a word to them because they could relate to the emotions I was experiencing. No doubt they were reliving, to some degree, their own story as they ministered to me in the midst of mine.

Brian held out his hand and gave me a small silver cross encased in an oval piece of acrylic. He said, "This helped get me through Austin, and I want you to have it."

Although it was just a small trinket, it meant the world to me. I would come to understand that it had no power of its own but that it could point me, time and again, to the All-Powerful One. For the next few months, it would keep reminding me of whose hands Elijah rested in as it found a home in my pocket.

I walked back towards the house and back upstairs

to Paige. She was pale from the blood loss, and the remaining medics were now preparing to transport her to the hospital as well. I asked about Elijah and was told they were flying him to Children's Hospital in Birmingham. I called my parents and asked them to go there since everyone else was headed to Montgomery.

About that time, one of the medics brought one of our dining chairs upstairs for Paige to sit in while they brought her downstairs. The gurney would not fit up the staircase, so they had to make do with what was available. After another ten minutes or so, we had Paige in the back of one of the ambulances, and Maddie Grace in the care of Mrs. Ann Key, one of the ladies from our church. I rode shotgun in the ambulance, and as we pulled out of my yard and drove up the driveway, I silently wondered, through a broken prayer, if Elijah was still alive.

CHAPTER 6

COMING APART AT THE SEAMS

Isaiah 43:2 (NIV)
"When you pass through the waters,
I will be with you;
and when you pass through the rivers,
they will not sweep over you.
When you walk through the fire,
you will not be burned;
the flames will not set you ablaze."

The ambulance driver was in no real hurry with Paige in the back. We mostly sat in silence as we rode down the highway towards Baptist South Hospital in Montgomery, the somber atmosphere feeling like that of a funeral home. Occasionally, I would hear the medic in the back talk to Paige, but up front, the two of us were quiet for the most part. The physical and emotional energy already spent left us all quiet and reserved, but the stillness of the moment was shattered just as we were leaving the Wetumpka city limits on Highway 231. I heard the medic in the back start to raise his voice at Paige, and then he started yelling at her, "Don't go to sleep! Stay with me! Stay with me!"

I jerked around to see what was going on and noticed that he was franticly trying to put in another IV. He looked up, his eyes wide with adrenaline, and shouted to the driver, "Go code 3! Go code 3!"

I had no idea what that meant but would later learn that he was telling the driver to turn on the lights and siren and go as fast as he could; in their lingo, it meant to "run emergency."

The driver shouted back, "We're not in the city yet!"

He was about to say something else but was cut off as the man in the back yelled again. "Go code 3! I'm losing her back here!"

As soon as those words were out, the driver flipped several switches on the dash and hammered the accelerator. The siren above our heads came to life and blared out as cars around us stopped. The vehicles in front of us pulled out of the way, and the engine roared in anger as we sped towards the hospital. The quietness was now a distant memory, and it seemed the entire vehicle was screaming around me. The driver started talking on the radio to his dispatcher, relaying information that the medic in the back shouted to him. It was chaos once again, and I felt as if my family was coming apart at the seams right in front of me, and there wasn't one thing I could do to make it stop.

A sense of desperation came over me as we ran through red lights and swerved around stopped cars. I had no control over what was happening, and it scared me to no end. I silently pleaded with God as the ambulance darted in and out of traffic. I thought Elijah was dead, so I begged him not to take Paige.

As the hospital finally came into view, I prayed, "Please God, take only one today. You can't have them both...you just can't."

As we came closer to Baptist South Hospital, I noticed the Air Evac helicopter on top of the building. Before I could ask, the driver told me that my son had been flown there instead of Children's in Birmingham. In that instant, I called my parents, who were en route to Birmingham, and had them come to Montgomery instead. I ended that call as the ambulance backed into the ER loading dock with Paige.

Jumping out of the ambulance, I ran to the back and saw several nurses and doctors waiting on the landing. Also, there was Tianna Gann, our Children's Minister from the church. Seeing a familiar face brought me comfort and instantly helped my mind recover from the trauma of the last few minutes.

Tianna Gann has always been a lot of fun to be around. She just happened to be in Montgomery that morning visiting hospitals and running other errands for the church. She was on her way back when she got the call to go to Baptist South. There was some misunderstanding about what had happened, but she went to Baptist South and found another member of our church, Kim Reinart.

Kim worked at the hospital and informed Tianna of what was happening. Not fully understanding the situation, Tianna patiently waited on the loading dock right outside of the ER with Kim. While she was standing there, other people started to congregate on the dock awaiting the arrival of the ambulance that was transporting Paige. One of these folks was the hospital chaplain. Once he knew who Tianna was, he began to talk to her, and as I understand it, he realized that she was not completely aware of the problems facing us that day.

As the casual conversation between them grew more serious, he finally asked her, "You do understand what is happening here, don't you?"

Tianna thought she did and replied, "I think so."

At that, the chaplain looked at her and realized that she hadn't received all of the information she needed to know. But before he could say anymore, Tianna asked him what he knew that she didn't. To which he replied, "There's more than a good chance that this man will lose both his wife and son today. It's that serious."

As soon as we arrived at the hospital, I jumped out of the passenger door like the Duke boys and ran to the rear of the ambulance. In the couple of seconds that it took, Paige was already out of the back and being rushed through the double sliding doors of the ER and down the hallways of the hospital. This was a scene from a medical drama on TV. It didn't seem real to me.

As soon as I had exited the ambulance, I made eye contact with Kim and Tianna, and I was relieved to see someone I knew. I'm not sure I can explain how comforting it was to know that I was not alone. I think this is what God had in mind when He inspired Paul to write Galatians 6:2. I have also heard it said, "When we take on the burdens of others we cut them in half. When we share in the joy of others it is multiplied."

I can attest to the truth in those statements. Ministry is a very messy process. It can be ugly, but it can also be one of the most rewarding experiences on this earth. None of my church family woke up that morning with the thought that they would love to help my family through one of the ugliest days of our lives; however, their love for us and our God caused their actions to line up with the faith they professed. It was one of the few beautiful moments of that day, and without them, I'm not sure I could have handled it.

A few minutes later, in a small corner of the E.R., the team of doctors and nurses stabilized Paige. It seemed that she was out of the woods. After another hour or so, they took her to a room upstairs in the hospital. There she went through the task of delivering the afterbirth, which weakened her all the more. By this time, most of our family had made it to Montgomery. A lot of our church family had also come to the hospital, but after finding that Paige was going to be ok, they all had the same question; *How is Elijah?*

There was a somberness and seriousness in Paige's room. Our family crowded into the small space, and there was a reverent silence that permeated the place. No one seemed to know what to say. It was just as quiet and still as the ambulance ride had been before Paige's vitals plummeted. Paige tried to rest her weakened body as best she could, and everyone else just seemed to be there, waiting for the bad news we expected to come. If anyone spoke, it was with a soft voice and a concerned expression. Once again, it was akin to being at a funeral. In short, we were all stunned and shocked.

Just two days before, on Saturday, our families had been at our house celebrating Maddie's second birthday. There was laughter and joy. Everything was wonderful and peaceful. We had all come together to not only rejoice over a birthday but to also put the memories of Maddie's long stay in the NICU behind us. We were a normal family, and we were about to add to it again. Everything would be routine this time, we thought, and we wouldn't have to travel that long, hard road in the NICU again.

About an hour or so later, we heard a knock at the door. My father opened it to find another doctor, a woman this time, at the door. She had a few people with her, all of them with somber-looking faces. I knew what this was. This was the moment we would find out that Elijah was dead. I didn't need to be told that because I had already begun to deal with his death in my mind. I had accepted the certainty of it, and I was already thinking about the future of our family. We would try for another baby, another son, again, if we could, or we would adopt if we had to. I would not let this be the end of my dream to father a son.

Once making their way inside the small, overcrowded room, the three of them stopped at the foot of Paige's hospital bed. We exchanged pleasantries, and they introduced themselves as doctors from the NICU. My stomach tightened as they talked, and I waited for the inevitable news they were about to share. She started talking about all they had done to try and save Elijah's life, and she explained the problems with having a child so early, especially at home. We knew all of this from our experience with Maddie, but we still listened, if for no other reason than to delay the bad news we knew was inevitable. But to my surprise, she kept using words in the present tense and not the past. Surely, he wasn't alive; there wasn't any way the child I saw loaded into that helicopter could survive. It wasn't possible!

She continued talking, explaining the lengths they had gone through with Elijah and closed by saying that he was hanging on to life, for now. My mind could not believe what my ears had just heard. Then she asked the question, "Do you want to go see him?"

A few minutes after the team of doctors had left, a nurse came inside the room with a wheelchair for Paige. We loaded her into it, and then she and I left the crowded room and made our way to the NICU to see our son together. I didn't want to think about the familiar road that lay ahead of us. I knew we were in for a battle. As we scrubbed our hands and arms once again, I wiped my mind clean of the hope that he would ever survive. For the second time that day, I had given up on my son and God's ability to save him.

A few hours earlier, as I watched the helicopter leave with him, I knew he was dead. I was still just as certain of that fact, so I tried to insulate my heart from the feelings it desperately wanted to feel. I couldn't have known that by making that choice, I would choose to force a struggle within myself to love my son unconditionally. This would be the beginning of a very dark time in my soul that I kept hidden from everyone else. I didn't want to acknowledge it, but I knew Paige wasn't the only member of our family to have given birth that day. I had birthed something of a demon that would continue to torment me throughout the next few years. I couldn't accept the situation for what it was, nor could I accept my son how he was. Those thoughts today make me sick with myself, and for a very long time, I have wished for the ability to live those moments over again.

Paige and I made our way across the NICU, feeling as if every nurse was staring at us. Finally, we came to Elijah's incubator on the far side of the large room and looked down on the youngest of us, fighting to survive. As Paige began to cry, I held on to her. I was stoic, numb to my feelings, and certain of the future. I could not allow myself to become emotionally attached to him as I had done with Maddie on the day she entered this world. I couldn't bear it!

One of the nurses came over and explained, in a quiet voice, what they were doing for him, and that his chances were slim at best. We knew that already, but just hearing those words again sent Paige back into tears. After fifteen minutes or so with him, we returned to Paige's room, where the rest of our family and friends waited.

Once back in the room, we told them about Elijah's condition. There were quiet sobs around the room but also the rejoicing that he was still alive. There was still hope in everyone else's mind, and that seemed to be enough for all of them. As for me, my heart was not as certain.

Elijah's birth weight was right at two pounds. When Paige and I saw him for the first time, without the cloud of panic and fear, we couldn't believe our eyes. He was small, extremely small. My hand would cover almost the entire length of his body. I wear a size 11.5 wedding ring, and it would easily slip over his hand, past his elbow, and up to his armpit. The sight of him hurt me, and to look on him, in that condition, brought pain to my soul. I took those feelings and shoved them into the hole I had created earlier. I buried them in his grave, the one I was sure he would occupy before very much longer.

I can't recall much more about that day in the hospital. There were a lot of people who came by to see Paige and show their support for us. Some of the folks from Mom and Dad's church came down to see her, and others from Paige's parent's church came as well. After Paige and I saw Elijah several more times, my family decided to go back to my house to get some rest, so we left the hospital that night around 8 pm.

Once back home, I found that Maddie had been entertained by Mrs. Ann Key the entire day. Mrs. Janice Sexton had also come to help, and I was thankful for their servant's heart. It may not have been much to them, but their simple act of babysitting allowed me time to be where I was needed. That's what God's people do, though, isn't it? We serve each other, and we love each other through the hardest of times. It doesn't have to be something spectacular. Sometimes it's just babysitting a two-year-old for a few hours.

Paige's mother and sister stayed with me that night, and the next morning we headed back down to the hospital. I expected to receive a call during the night about Elijah, but I didn't. He was still alive, and I wondered how long he could hold on. My parents went back home to Pell City to await my brother Jeff's arrival from Georgia because he was going to stay with them a night before coming down to my house.

My brother and I are very close. He is two years older than me, and we have a very strong bond. He made a career out of the Navy, so we didn't get to spend that much time together anymore, but we always talked on the phone. Even when his service to our country took his family to Guam, we still spoke at least once a week. I love him as much as one man can love another, and there is nothing one of us wouldn't do for the other. I was looking forward to his visit with us because he is one of the only people on this earth that I can bare my soul to without any fear of judgment.

Once back at the hospital, we found Paige had made an outstanding recovery from her trauma the day before. Her color was back to normal, and she was already asking to be discharged. She's never been one to sit around, so I knew if she were anywhere near 100%, they'd have a hard time holding on to her.

Once again, we went into the NICU to see Elijah, and this time we got to take Maddie with us. Paige and I held her up so that she could see her little brother through the clear plastic walls of the incubator. She stared at him silently with her face and hands pressed against the warm plastic. She was in awe of him, and I could clearly see the love flowing from her eyes. After a few minutes, she quietly asked us some questions about him and the different machines he was hooked up to. We answered them as best we could, but I'm sure we never fully satisfied her curiosity.

That afternoon, Paige was discharged from the hospital, and her sister and mother went back home as my brother and his family arrived at our house. The next few days involved more trips to the hospital as Elijah's condition worsened. I thought the end for him was near, and I remember stating as much to my brother and his wife one night on our way home from the hospital. The certainty and lack of emotion with which I spoke about it scared me, but there wasn't anything I felt I could do to change it. I was simply waiting on the tragedy I knew was inevitable.

As the days wore on, I encountered a problem that most people share during times like this. Information. How do you get it out, and how do you keep people updated when it changes? Elijah's condition changed daily, sometimes even hourly, so there was always the "latest news." After hearing several things at church that weren't true or were days old, I decided to act. I took one of the phone lines in my office at work and put voice mail on it. I gave the number out to everyone who asked about him, and it was also shared on the announcements at our church, both in the worship guide and on the projector screens. For those who wanted to keep up with Elijah, they could call that number and hear my voice detailing his condition. I updated this line every night before bedtime and sometimes several times during the day. It was a great way to keep everyone up to date who wanted to be in the loop. As I was doing the simple things that made our lives easier, God was working to show us Himself in ways we never thought of.

Over the next few weeks, as Elijah continued to deteriorate, we began to lose confidence in the doctors at the hospital. They were doing all they had been trained to do, but with Paige's sister, Brandi, working at Children's in Birmingham, we knew there was more that could be done. We celebrated Thanksgiving as best we could that year, but by the following Monday, November 27th, things at the hospital had reached the boiling point for us.

Elijah had been diagnosed with a grade 4 brain bleed, and it had not resolved on its own, as Maddie's had done. The soft spot on the top of his head had begun to bulge from the pressure inside. Time was critical, and one of the doctors there wanted to "tap" his head to relieve the pressure. This involved sticking a needle into his head and drawing off the excess fluid with a syringe. Of course, this would not solve anything and would have to be repeated, again and again.

Brandi and Paige had visited Elijah that morning but would not give consent for the procedure to be done. They wanted him transferred to Children's instead. I also wanted that, but when the doctor called me, he explained that he had already called Children's and there simply wasn't any room available for Elijah at the moment. Exhausted from being the go-between and ready to see anything done to benefit my son, I gave him permission to go ahead with the procedure. I felt guilty for it, but I also felt as if I had no other choice.

I called Paige and relayed to her the information and the decision I had made. She exploded into tears and anger. We all knew that more could be done at Children's, but we couldn't get him there. After talking with her for a few minutes and taking a verbal scolding, I called the doctor back and told him that we had changed our minds and could no longer consent to the procedure. Brandi, meanwhile, was making phone calls of her own that would soon prove to be the difference in the life or death of our son.

About thirty minutes or so later, Paige called me back. She was much calmer and brighter than before, and she explained that Brandi had been able to arrange a miracle. Brandi had called one of her co-workers at Children's, and somehow a nurse practitioner, Linda Vest, had gotten involved.

After hearing of Elijah's condition, the treatment the doctors were considering, and knowing our family, Linda Vest made a phone call to the hospital in Montgomery. I wasn't there to hear it, but from what I have gathered secondhand, the conversation was one-sided for the most part. Linda told them in no uncertain terms that they were not to lay another finger on our son and that Children's Hospital transport was on their way to get him. I wish I could have eavesdropped on that call. I smile just thinking about it.

After hearing the news, I asked Brandi what kind of an ambulance Elijah would be riding in. Apparently, it is some kind of big-rig-type vehicle that is a mobile NICU. I learned later that day that it is staffed by some of the most courteous people you could ask for when they called our home to let me know that they had taken custody of Elijah. It was already near midnight, and the call had jarred me from my slumber. A couple of hours later, the phone rang again, this time letting us know that Elijah was at Children's Hospital and was in stable condition.

We were to be at Children's Hospital on November 29th anyway, because Maddie had to have surgery on her ears. She was prone to ear infections, and they were going to put tubes in her ears. Paige and Maddie stayed at her mother's house that evening; then, I met them at Children's the next day for Maddie's procedure. It might not have played on anyone else's mind but having both of my children in the same hospital felt overwhelming. I didn't feel as if I could give enough attention, thought, or prayer to either one of them, so I eventually just prayed, *God, have your way.*

Once Elijah was at Children's, they began running every possible test to learn all they could about his current condition. After being evaluated by the doctors at Children's, it was determined that Elijah needed to have a shunt placed in his head to alleviate the pressure from clogged ventricles. It's a difficult thing to explain, but your brain has four ventricles, or areas filled with fluid, under your brain. These areas drain fluid through a narrow opening at the back of the base of your brain. When a brain bleed occurs and blood clots, it can prevent these tiny holes from draining. Then, the fluid builds, and pressure increases until it is relieved. The Montgomery doctors wanted to draw the fluid out with a syringe, but at Children's, they place a "shunt," a one-way valve, with a line allowing the fluid to drain from the brain and back into the body elsewhere. This surgery was scheduled for Friday, December 1st and couldn't come soon enough for all of us. Although my heart still yearned for my son to live, I still didn't have the confidence that he would.

That Friday, all our immediate family came to the hospital. It wasn't a lengthy procedure, and the doctor who later came out to talk to us was extremely personable and kind. He took his time, explained everything to us, and let us know that the surgery was a success. A few hours later, we were permitted to see him, and even though it hadn't been long, we all could see an immediate improvement in him. He wasn't just surviving anymore. There were regular movements, and he acted more like a baby. I know that's a strange thing to say, but if you could have seen him during the first few weeks of his life, you would understand just what I am trying to describe.

During Elijah's first few weeks of life, his condition never once improved. Every time we received news, it was bad, and every time we went to see him, he had worsened. That begins to take a toll on you as a parent, and it's hard to accurately put into words the desperation you feel as you watch your child slowly fade into nothingness. His appearance was terrible. He wasn't able to eat, so he was skin and bones. Any fatty birth weight was gone after a few days, and Elijah's only source of nourishment came through the IV line that was placed into the remnants of his umbilical cord in his navel.

He would shake uncontrollably, and his movements were only that of a seizure or other unintentional consequence. He simply wasn't there.

All of that changed immediately following his shunt surgery. Elijah looked more like a child, his movements were that of a baby, and for the first time, a small glimmer of hope appeared. It wasn't much, but for the NICU parents out there reading this, you know how each small victory is truly celebrated.

Over the next few weeks, we drove to see Elijah as much as we possibly could. Usually, Paige would go up on Tuesdays and Thursdays, and then we would all go on Saturdays. Sometimes Paige would make the ninety-mile drive only to find the NICU shut down for visitors because a child lay dead or dying within its walls. The family of that child was allowed the dignity of having the opportunity to say goodbye to their precious one in private, without the eyes of everyone else on them. While this was inconvenient for us, we understood completely. Who knows when that might be our family behind the closed doors of grief and loss?

It was during one of Paige's weekly visits, sometime just before Christmas, that she was finally able to hold Elijah for the first time since the day of his birth. It would be another couple of weeks before I had the same opportunity because of the process it took to remove him and all the machinery in the incubator. It was neither a short nor an easy process, but it was rewarding.

During this time, we relied heavily, once again, on Paige's sister, Brandi, to keep us updated. Although she couldn't be assigned to him as his nurse, she kept up with him nonetheless. This was altogether different than when Maddie was in the NICU at Baptist East in Montgomery. We had an inside source here: someone who could give us the latest results from the tests, even before the doctors got them. To say that she was a blessing would be an understatement, so I'll just use the word *angel*. She was like an angel watching over our son.

Even as Elijah continued to improve, there were still occasional setbacks. I continued to update the voicemail regularly, letting everyone who cared to know the condition of our son. During some of the more challenging days, I sat alone in my office, with tears of sorrow streaming down my face, questioning how we'd ever make it through this terrible nightmare. During these times, the phone line I had set up with the voicemail would ring a short "chirp" ring that would let me know someone was calling to check on Elijah. There was one particularly tough day when all hope seemed lost, and I felt all alone and depressed. I began to wallow in the mud of self-pity; consequently, before long, I was soiled to my soul in a selfish depression that told me we were never going to pull through this. It was then, through the blessing of a voicemail, that God showed me once again how much He loves me. The chirp ring of the phone sounded like a full-blown herd of crickets at dusk, and I was reminded that on the other end of every one of those calls was someone who cared about Elijah, my family, and me. My family was loved, not just by God but also by those he had placed around us. They were doing just as Jesus said they should when He spoke in John 13:35:

> *"By this everyone will know that you are my disciples, if you love one another."*

When everything around me screamed sadness and regret, I was shaken awake by the chirping alarm clock of love and joy. God was being generous with us in our time of need, and He was indeed placing His joy in our hearts.

Elijah was doing so well by the end of January that he was finally moved to the third floor of Children's hospital, to their version of the "well side" of the NICU. He began eating from a bottle and acting more and more like the baby we had prayed for. It was during this time that we were shattered to learn that Elijah was blind. Because of his premature birth, there was a problem with his optic nerves; therefore, it was determined by the specialist that Elijah would most likely never be able to see the beautiful world around him.

While this may not seem as big of a deal to everyone else, it was to me. If you remember, my dreams included baseball, racing, football, and everything else that brought fame and fortune to my boy's life. How was that going to happen if he was blind? At this news, I retreated once again into the hole I had created the day he was born. It was filled with darkness and devoid of any hope that my son could one day make his own mark on this great big world.

Paige was equally devastated by this news, but to her credit, she seemed better able to deal with it than I could. I tried to hide it and thought I did a good job of it, but later learned that she knew the truth all along. She seemed to understand that this was just another challenge to overcome, another opportunity for God to show His greatness and goodness to us. But, at that time, I wasn't as optimistic or as full of faith as she was.

Once Elijah had proven himself to the doctors, we were finally able to bring him home on March 7, 2007, some four months after being born. We would have several therapists coming to work with him. He would be on oxygen, and there were other life-changing circumstances that came home with him. But we were overjoyed to have him home and to try to regain some sense of normalcy.

After a month or so, we had settled into a routine again. Our lives were starting to adjust to a new normal that included visits to the doctor, in-home physical therapy, and other services that would help our son grow and thrive. Paige and Maddie seemed to always be on the go, taking Elijah to one appointment or another. At the end of March, Elijah was hospitalized again, but this time only for a few days. It began a period of adjustment to the "new normal" of having a child with special needs.

On Sunday, April 22, 2007, we took Elijah to church for the first time. As you would imagine, he was quite the celebrity. Everyone marveled at the tiny miracle before them, and a week later, our church had a welcome home party for Elijah, complete with cake and ice cream. The entire church celebrated with us because they had "borne our burdens as if they were their own." Elijah belonged to them too, and our entire congregation praised God for the miracle He had worked. They had prayed for him, celebrated each milestone, and cried over each setback. They were invested in his life, not necessarily with money, but with time spent before our King in prayer for Elijah. They shored up my family as we endured one of the most difficult times of our lives. I remember being humbled that Sunday night by the overwhelming love shown to my family.

Something still was not right within me, however, and even though I tried to hide it, it still came out in fits and spurts. I still had a hard time accepting that God had allowed Elijah to be like he was. Looking back, I can see that I was very angry at God, but I did not know a way to fully process that anger. That anger came out, not in fits of rage, but in silence and emotional abandonment. I did everything I could to avoid the billboard of love God had blessed my life with. Elijah's struggles challenged my view of who God is and what God's nature is. I did not understand how a loving God could allow a child to go through all that Elijah had. So, instead of facing the issue head-on, I avoided it altogether by not taking a genuine interest in my son. If I were given a choice of whom to take care of, it would be Maddie. I reasoned that Paige knew how to take care of Eli better anyway, and I would just get in the way.

As soon as I got home from work, I began working on or around our home. Paige usually cooked every meal with Elijah in her arms as I was going about making our house a beautiful place to live. In retrospect, I should have turned my focus to making the heart of my home, my family, more beautiful, instead of worrying about what the outside of it looked like. Like the Pharisees of Jesus' time, I was more concerned with the outside appearance than the inward beauty of both my relationship with Jesus and my home.

Do not mistake these actions for lack of love on my part. I loved my son, just not for who God had created him to be. I loved him because he was my flesh and blood, and I showed that love to Eli every chance I got. It was a great paradox in my life—how I could love someone so much but still not fully give all my heart away in that love. I guess that I must have still been waiting for the other shoe to drop, so to speak, not understanding that the time I had was limited.

Months went by, and the routine of life became more set. In September of 2007, we were interviewed by Mike Royer, a reporter for NBC13 in Birmingham. The "Spirit of Alabama" was a part of the 10 pm newscast every Thursday night. It usually involved a feel-good story from the local area. Somehow, Mr. Royer received our information, so we sat down with Elijah to be interviewed about his life.

This was not a first for us. Eli had made the papers on a couple of different occasions. His birth, and the response of the Deputy Sheriffs that day, had made the Montgomery Advertiser, our local paper. After he came home, we were invited to the airport to meet with John Fryer, the flight nurse on the Air Evac helo that transported him to the hospital that day. There was a reporter there, as well, who captured the reunion and wrote an article about it for the same paper. I remember that day well, as Mr. Fryer shared his side of the story concerning the day Elijah entered this world.

CHAPTER 7

SOFTENING A HEART

Ezekiel 36:26 (NIV)
"I will give you a new heart and put a new spirit
in you; I will remove from you your heart of stone
and give you a heart of flesh."

I wasn't sure what to expect as Paige and I arrived at the Wetumpka airport, but I knew that I would be glad to see Mr. Fryer again, this time under better circumstances. I wanted to shake the man's hand who had helped save Elijah's life, and I also wanted to introduce him to Paige and Maddie as well.

We pulled up outside the hanger where the helicopter was stored, and we were met by a reporter from the Montgomery Advertiser, as well as John, who was on duty in his flight suit. After a few pictures beside the helicopter and answering some questions, I finally had the chance to talk to Mr. Fryer privately, and the story he told amazed me. It further cemented the fact that God was already at work that day, even before any of us were ever aware of the nightmare to come.

John began by telling me that meeting us was a privilege. He rarely gets to see any of the patients he treats, and it was nice to see how well Elijah was doing.

I had never thought of how hard it must be to be a flight nurse on one of those helicopters. They see the worst injuries and people at their most desperate in their struggle for life. I'm sure there's very little reward for their work, so, looking back, I can see a little glimpse of the gift we were able to give him that day.

Mr. Fryer started recalling the day my son was born, from his perspective, and the more he spoke, the more I saw God's hand. The helicopter was already in the air when the call came in for them to come get Elijah. They had flown to Tennessee to get a repair part for the chopper and were only a few miles away when dispatched to our home. He shared that although they were low on fuel, they could divert long enough to transport Elijah. I asked who decided not to take him immediately to Children's Hospital in Birmingham because I thought that was a crucial mistake made that morning. The mistake in my mind was God's providence. As Mr. Fryer spoke, he dropped his head, and looked towards the ground. He said that he had made that decision while they were fueling the helicopter at the airport. Elijah would have never made it to Birmingham, so he diverted to Montgomery. The kicker is that without the time spent refueling the helicopter, he wouldn't have had enough time to evaluate Elijah. They would have simply lifted off from my house and flown to Birmingham, and Elijah would have died mid-air. Because they had to refuel, he had more time to see just how critical Elijah's condition was.

Looking back up at me, our eyes meeting, Mr. Fryer said, "I'll never forget the look on your face that day."

Through welling tears, I asked him what he meant by

that, and he told me that he could sense the desperation in my voice and see the love I had for my newborn son in my eyes. I was taken aback by his words. He was reminding me, without knowing it, that I possessed a deep love and acceptance for Elijah regardless of how angry his handicapped condition made me at God. I had chosen to bury those emotions, and it was as if God Himself was picking at the scab beneath the makeshift bandage of denial and anger.

After finding Paige, Maddie, and Elijah still talking to the reporter, we were given a tour of the little shack the crew uses on their workdays. There wasn't much to it, and it reminded me a lot of the berthing compartments I slept in while on a ship in the Navy. A few minutes later, we were back in our car driving home; and although we talked a lot about the events of the day, my mind was still busy digesting the words John Fryer had spoken to me. Unfortunately, I didn't allow those words to permeate into my heart and start to break loose the chains that imprisoned me.

As more time passed, Elijah continued to improve; however, he was still developmentally delayed. On the first Saturday of November 2007, we celebrated his first birthday, along with Maddie's third, at our home with family and friends. My Aunt Sharon made cakes for both of them, and the day was filled with laughter and joy. We talked about the long road both had traveled down, and we celebrated our miracles as a testament to the goodness of our God.

Even though Elijah was now a year old, he was developmentally a 5-month-old. He couldn't sit up on his own, and he was still eating from a bottle. He was given physical therapy, as well as other therapies, that would hopefully help him to begin eating, eventually crawling, and possibly walking. Unfortunately, these delays were more ammunition for the army of demons in my mind. With every thought about what he could not do, I further suppressed all that he had overcome.

In early 2008, our Pastor's wife, Mrs. Jane Miller, gave me a CD to listen to. She said that she thought I would like it and felt that I needed to hear it.

The musician's name is Gordon Mote. He hails from Gadsden, Alabama; even though he is blind, he plays the piano and sings beautifully. I'm not sure Mrs. Jane could know that the gift she was giving would be used to start a transformation in my life, but that's exactly what happened.

I downloaded the CD onto my MP3 player and started listening to it the very next morning as I was running laps in our field. All was going well until I heard the song, "Don't Let Me Miss the Glory." Tears began to run down my face as I ran, and before long, I had to stop and catch my breath between the sobs of emotion.

"A blind man was singing this!" I thought.

Somehow, through Mr. Mote's song, I drew a straight line between Elijah's blindness and the fact that I was missing the glory of God Himself in my son's life. Guilt and shame began to filter into my conscience, and for the first time since Elijah's birth, I began to dream big dreams for my son once again. Baseball, football, and racing dreams gave way to a yet undetermined destiny of whatever God saw fit. As Mr. Mote continued to sing, visions of my son's now bright future began to take shape in my mind. I had begun to think about

Elijah's life and God's will for him, and as I did, a small voice started to whisper in my heart. I knew what I had to do, but I wasn't sure how to go about asking God for the forgiveness my soul needed. I thought the road back to Him would include backtracking through the potholes I had hit so far, but I had a lot to learn about true repentance. The fact is that once we admit to our sins, no matter how great, the blood of Jesus fills every crack and pothole. It's simply a matter of trusting that God has done what He promised to do in Scripture.

A month or so later, at another doctor's office, we received some good news about Elijah's vision. We were told that his vision would likely improve to 20/800, and that would mean that he might be able to see something other than light and darkness.

By June of 2008, at 18 months old, Elijah was finally gaining some traction in his development. He still wasn't sitting up on his own or eating any solid food, but there were minor improvements here and there. The best thing was that we finally weren't going backward. I still hadn't gotten my heart right with God regarding my son, and I was still struggling with my role as a father to a special needs boy. All of that was about to change, however, and it would happen in a most unexpected place.

CHAPTER 8

UNCONDITIONAL LOVE

1 John 1:9 (NIV)
"If we confess our sins, he is faithful and just
and will forgive us our sins and purify us from all
unrighteousness."

Paige has always been the crafty type. No, I do not mean that she is a manipulator. I mean that she has always liked putting her creativity into her hands and working with different forms of art. She has painted and worked with clay, glass fusing, bead making, and several other forms of arts and crafts.

I have always encouraged her to pursue whatever she wanted and have tried to support her work in any way possible. So, in the first week of June 2008, I arranged for her to take a class on a kind of glass crafting that she was interested in. The course was just outside of Atlanta, Georgia, so we had reserved a hotel room for one night and started making plans concerning what I would do with Maddie and Elijah while she was in class.

The first order of business in our plan was making sure that whatever hotel we stayed in had a pool. Both of our children loved the water, so we made sure that wherever we ended up that Friday night, we would be swimming in a pool. After checking out the next morning, I would drop Paige off at her class, and then the kids and I were on our own until 5 that evening, trying to find something to do with the time on our hands.

Paige had asked me repeatedly if I would be ok, and I had always told her I would. It bothered me that she thought I couldn't handle them for eight hours on my own, but the fact that she was right to be worried bothered me even more. I was still not the father I needed to be, and she knew it.

On Friday night, June 6th, we were all in the hotel pool, just as I thought we would be. Fortunately, we had the small indoor pool to ourselves, so we were able to have as much fun as we could stand. Maddie, in her floaties, would stand on the side of the pool, hold her hands in the air, and shout, "One, Two, Three, Four!" and then jump in. She would paddle to the ladder and repeat the process as I held Elijah in front of me in the water. Sometimes Maddie would lose count and start over. That made Paige and me laugh that much harder as we saw the great time she was having. But she wasn't the only one enjoying herself. I had found a good deal of joy in holding Elijah out in front of me as my grandfather had done for me so many years ago.

Paige came over a few times to ask if I was ready to let her have him, but after telling her no each time, she finally just stopped asking. I think she could sense something going on within me but just wasn't sure what it was. Maybe she couldn't believe that I was finally taking a genuine interest in our son. Whatever it was, she knew to leave well enough alone; and, Elijah and I enjoyed the rest of our time playing in the water, having a great time, father and son.

The following morning, I had a foreboding feeling in my stomach. As I dropped Paige off at her class, I smiled a fake smile and tried to reassure her that we would be fine.

With that said, you need to understand that I am very capable of taking care of almost any child for a day or two, but Elijah presented several problems that I had not yet learned to solve. The first of which, and the most important, was his attachment to Paige. When he wanted her, he would scream to the top of his lungs. His face would turn beet red, and the ear-piercing cries would not stop until Paige picked him up and began to talk to him. I was of no use. Sometimes, on rare occasions, I could sing *his* song, "Jesus Loves Me," and it would buy a few minutes of peace before he started afresh his screaming and crying. If this sort of thing were to happen on this day, I'm not sure what I could do. So, as I pulled back into the busy suburban Atlanta traffic, I began to pray that God would give us a good day. I didn't know that God's plans *were* for a great day, a life-changing day.

Our first stop of the day was at the local shopping mall. We had borrowed a tandem stroller from some church friends, so I loaded Maddie in the back, Elijah in the front, and we rolled our happy caravan through the mall's glass door entrance.

Without any plans, we simply strolled around the mall, occasionally going into a store and killing the time we had. I thought a movie would be good for us after lunch and had already looked up the showtimes at a movie theater not far away. As we rolled around the mall,

I noticed people looking at Elijah, smiling at Maddie and me, and commenting on how cute they both were. When Elijah got hungry, the attention from other people intensified because I had Maddie lean over to feed him from the back seat of the stroller as I continued to walk, pushing them around the mall. She loved it, he loved it; so, as I walked on, I began to wonder why I had such a hard time accepting Elijah while everyone else didn't. That thought kept being weighed against the constant smiles of every stranger we met until the Holy Spirit's conviction grabbed ahold of my heart in a vise-like grip. With every step I took, the need for repentance and acceptance grew until I could take it no more.

Almost in a fit of emotion, the chaos in my heart was broken, as Maddie interrupted, "Daddy, Bubba has a stinky."

We were close to a mall map, so I looked through tear-laden eyes for the nearest restroom. We weren't far away; so, I hurried towards the end of the passageway before Elijah could start crying or anyone could see my now swollen and welled eyes. I was thankful that my mind and heart had a break from the crushing pressure God was placing on it. But as we found the crowded restroom, I reached down into the stroller to pick up Elijah, and the second wave of conviction came crashing in.

Elijah smiled as I picked him up, and as I told Maddie to stand towards the wall with her eyes closed, the hardness of my heart started to break. I placed Elijah on the changing table as urinals and toilets flushed behind me. I unsnapped his outfit and pulled loose the straps on his diaper; then, all at once, my heart was undone.

I dropped my head as tears took flight from my eyes. I began to silently pray for forgiveness and then admit to the sins of a father that had placed too much importance on what he thought his son should be instead of who his son was created to be. The more I prayed and cried, the more the Holy Spirit tightened His grip. Before I knew it, I was on my knees on the filth of the floor, confessing and repeating aloud the secrets I had kept hidden. My right hand was raised, and as I steadied Elijah on the table with my left hand, I felt Maddie place her head on my back. She embraced me from the side and began to pat my shoulder with her right hand. I heard the footsteps of other men as they walked behind me. I wonder now what they must have thought, but at that moment, I didn't care.

After a few minutes of what some would call prayer, I opened my eyes and looked at my son. He looked at me, as best he could, a half-smile on his face. As I stood up to change the old diaper, he beheld a new Daddy with what little vision he had. I looked around and noticed two other men who were trying not to stare, so I finished changing Elijah's diaper, wiped my eyes, loaded both of my children back in the stroller, and opened the door to push it through. The man that emerged from that dirty restroom was much different than the one who went in.

The three of us ate lunch in the mall's food court and left for the movie theater shortly afterward. Elijah had been great, and he hadn't had any tantrums yet. We pulled into the theater parking lot, and this time I left the stroller in the car as we headed inside to watch "Kung Fu Panda."

Inside the theater, I tried to sit in an area that would allow us to leave without disturbing anyone if we needed to. The movie began, and I found myself with an unexpected happiness and a relieved peacefulness. There was a contentment with my life and my son, and I was beginning to finally accept that the narrow road was one worth traveling, even if it meant that the dreams I had carried for so long had to die.

After an hour or so, the movie's evil character scared Maddie, so we decided to leave since Elijah was starting to get a little fussy anyway. Once back at the car, I loaded them into their car seats, and we drove around for the remaining time as we waited for Paige.

A little after 5 o'clock, we arrived to find Paige leaving her class right on time. As she got into the car, she asked about our day, and Maddie was more than happy to fill her in on our little adventure. To Maddie's credit, she never mentioned the chaos in the men's room. Her main attention had been re-focused on the movie and the characters in it. I didn't mention it, either. I thought I would just let the Lord work through me and have my actions and attitude reveal the difference. In truth, I wasn't sure of what had just happened or the ramifications of what God had begun just hours earlier.

A couple of hours later, we pulled back into the driveway and settled into our Saturday evening routine. The next day was church, and as involved as we have always been, that meant that we took very few Sundays off.

Looking back, I'm not sure when Paige noticed the difference in me because we never talked specifically about it. She did bring it up in Brother Larry's office as we met with both him and Mrs. Charleen a few years later. That's another story for another time. I don't want to get too far ahead of myself. God still has a lot more showing off to do.

Chapter 9

PROJECTS

Proverbs 3:5-6 (NIV)
"Trust in the Lord with all your heart and lean
not on your own understanding; in all your ways
submit to him, and he will make your paths
straight."

I previously mentioned the work we have done on our home before. I have always been one to have some kind of project going on, and the more challenging the work, the better. In the Navy, even though my job was not a physically difficult one, I would volunteer to scrape the floor of a bathroom or perform some other kind of improvement project around the ship.

Our first home in Leeds, AL needed a complete renovation, so, in the month or so before we married, our parents joined us. We did everything imaginable to the place to make it the beautiful little house of our dreams. The log home we bought in the Santuck community a few years later was in even worse condition. Paige and I, as well as our parents, again worked countless weekends and weeknights, trying to transform it into something we could be proud of.

I usually made a project list and planned out what

I would try to accomplish each day. I wrote this daily list in ink in the calendar I kept so that I could not erase it. Whatever I had written down had to be done, plain and simple. Looking back at this insanity, I can clearly see, often through teary eyes, the time these daily projects robbed from my family. I thought that we'd all be happy when they were finished, not understanding that true happiness is found in the moment and cannot be planned.

After that fateful day in the men's room, my project list was trimmed, and I began to write in pencil. Even with that, I started carrying a big eraser along with my calendar, keeping track of what we *had* done the day before instead of what I had planned to do. Before long, as we realized that Elijah's condition would require special attention, I thought of ways my projects and my family could co-exist.

On one of my daily calls with my brother, talking about all of the work around the house, I stated, "My plan is to build Elijah a handicapped bathroom in the basement."

I think this may have been the first time I admitted to anyone, including myself, the extent that Elijah's life would impact our own.

In the past, I had been scared that we would become "those people." You know the ones I am talking about. They are the families who have nothing, materially speaking, because of the health of one or more of their children. Their lives are spent as caretakers of their child who will never improve. Once the parents die, the burden of care is shifted to either another family member or to a special home of some kind.

I didn't want this for us, and the potential burden was more than I thought I could bear. Questions surrounded that life and ended with answers I didn't have or want to acknowledge. Who would care for Elijah after we died? How could we ensure the care and safety of our son after we were gone? Likewise, any thought of Paige and me quietly retiring and doing whatever we wanted was also dead. In short, the future was anything but certain, and that fact scared me until I had confessed it to God that day in the mall. After that, I was able to walk in the moment God had prepared for me and trust that He would handle the future, no matter what it held. There is great release and peace in knowing that you don't have to have all the answers and that you're not in control.

I look back on the days spent afterward, and I saw myself looking for ways to enjoy my son regardless of what that meant. No, he would never fulfill the superficial dreams I had before, but that didn't matter anymore. He was my son, and I loved him. Not for what I thought he *should* be, but for who he was. *Who he was.*

That may not sound like much to you, but accepting my son was one of the hardest, most spiritually challenging times of my life. To see him as he was, with his physical and mental handicaps, challenged all I thought I knew about who God is. The two could not coexist in my mind before that fateful day in the mall. Afterward, I stopped trying to make sense of any of it, and I simply loved my son. Somehow Elijah's handicaps and the goodness of God started dancing together in ways that I once thought impossible. I finally realized that God gifted him to me and me to him...me to him.

I'm not sure I thought about that second part until after I had been on my knees on the filth of the floor, confessing the ugly stain on my soul.

Something tells me to stop right here. You may be reading this from the very situation I am describing. Your life may be defined by the care you give your special needs child. You may have the same questions and concerns that I did, unable to fully digest the path your life is on. You may be mad at God or feel trapped by the enormity of the task at hand. I have only one thing that I can say: Don't give up. Keep fighting and believing. I know firsthand how hard the days can be, and I know that God can be enough if you let Him. Live in the moment as best you can, and trust that He will give you strength and energy for tomorrow. As for today, give everything you have. Don't leave an ounce of energy on the table. You're not promised tomorrow.

As the summer of 2008 came to a close, we spent most of our Labor Day weekend at Paige's family's lake house in Pell City. We came back for church on Sunday and decided to stay home after church instead of returning to the lake as we usually did. The next day, Labor Day, the four of us drove over to Pine Mountain, Georgia, and spent the day at the Wild Animal Safari. We took our time looking at the animals and simply enjoyed each other's company on the beautiful day God blessed us with. Elijah was growing up, and that day was one that I finally stepped back and marveled at all we had been through.

CHAPTER 10

THE COMING STORM

Romans 8:18
"I consider that our present sufferings are not
worth comparing with the glory that will be
revealed in us."

In the early months of 2008, Paige's mother, Donna, became sick again. She had battled ovarian cancer a couple of years before, but it was in the summer of 2008 that it returned. She was hospitalized several times, but by Labor Day, she was not doing well and didn't leave the house very often. We were all still hopeful, even though her diabetes made her recovery that much more difficult. By the end of September, Donna's health had declined to the point that Hospice had been called in, and as if that weren't enough, Elijah's shunt malfunctioned, and he had to have surgery to place a new one. As the year matured into October, we found two family members struggling once again with their health.

Elijah had another neurology appointment on October 1st to check the newly placed shunt and to make sure that it was doing the job of allowing the fluid of his brain to drain back into his body. At this appointment, the doctor did not like what he saw, so Elijah was admitted once again to Children's Hospital and scheduled for yet another shunt surgery the following day.

Elijah's surgery on Thursday, October 2nd, went smoothly, and Maddie came back home with me as Paige stayed with Elijah in the hospital. I took Maddie to work with me the next day, and I think she enjoyed the change in her routine. We went out for lunch, bought groceries after work, and had a great time just hanging out together. You'd be surprised how much fun you can have at work with a little girl who is about to turn 4.

On Saturday, Paige and Eli were discharged, and our family was once again whole. Elijah was scheduled for a follow-up visit with his pediatrician, Dr. Fekete, the following Monday, so we enjoyed the rest of the weekend, thinking that we had experienced the last of our health problems for a while.

The next day, Elijah was once again fussy and agitated, and it seemed that this latest shunt surgery had not worked as well as we had hoped. Once at Dr. Fekete's office, we were given another appointment for him at Children's Hospital the following day.

That day, Tuesday, October 7th, Elijah was admitted to the hospital once again so that the doctors could run the necessary tests to see exactly what was ailing our son. He couldn't speak, so his only way of communicating what was wrong with him was screaming. By this time, he had had not been himself for several weeks, and we had noticed that we simply could not make him happy. He was uncomfortable with something, and it was up to the doctors to find that out.

That evening I took Maddie to the State Fair in Montgomery. We rode roller coasters, played games, and had a great time together. We were working our way down the midway when Paige called to tell me that their long day resulted in Elijah's admittance. I could hear the exhaustion in her voice; however, I had hoped that this was nothing serious and that they would both be home the next day.

That following morning, Elijah's condition had worsened. He had screamed most of the night, and only the strongest of pain medicine had helped the two of them to rest. If you've never had your child admitted to the hospital at this age, you really can't appreciate the direness of the situation. Paige may as well have been admitted to the hospital herself. Someone had to be there with him, holding him, speaking for him, and since it is 100 miles away for us, it's not easy to switch out jobs. If you factor in the fact that I am the sole breadwinner, then it really is not a question as to who would have to stay with him. So, for all intents and purposes, Paige is confined to the hospital, bedridden with our son.

That night at church, everyone asked about them and continued their support of us in prayer. Several people asked about keeping Maddie while I went to work, but I didn't trust just anyone with our oldest child. Our closest friends at the time, Jonathan and Christy Stuart, kept Maddie a few hours that day and would also help us through the days and weeks that followed. But that night, I simply smiled, thanked them for their concern and prayers, and reiterated that this was just a bump in the road. How was I to know that in less than 24 hours, my son would be fighting for his very life?

The next day, I took Maddie to work with me as

Paige saw Elijah through more tests and endless frustration. Elijah had started to have mini-seizures, and as Paige tried to tell a couple of the doctors about it, they either didn't believe her or passed off his convulsions as evidence of something else. That night, Elijah's seizures worsened. As his condition grew more dire, he was transferred to the ICU and awaited another shunt surgery the next day. By the end of the evening, my usually quiet and reserved wife became something of a "Mama Bear." Paige had thrown one doctor out of the room and had found a voice she never knew she possessed.

The next day, I took a personal day from work because Elijah was scheduled for yet another shunt surgery. It was determined that this latest shunt, less than two weeks old, had also malfunctioned and that the pressure on his brain had caused all the symptoms he was experiencing. I still had questions. Why did these two shunts fail so quickly? Was it a problem with Elijah or with the shunt? Those questions could not be answered just yet, so Paige and Elijah were kept in the hospital until more tests could be run to determine the root of the problem. Until the doctors could figure it out, Elijah's shunt was bypassed, and both he and Paige would be confined to a hospital bed once he was released back to a regular room.

During this time, I sent out emails to people detailing Elijah's condition, and just like when he was born, information became a problem. This time, instead of voicemail, I used email. I didn't think this would be as long of an ordeal as his birth had been, so I didn't see the need for mass communication yet. Fortunately, April

Sexton did, and she started a CaringBridge.org page for Elijah on October 11th. She simply posted my emails until I started posting them myself a few days later. This next chapter will contain that communication, as well as my commentary on it, so that I can accurately describe the chaos that slowly enveloped my family.

CHAPTER 11

TWO VERSES IN THE SAME SAD SONG

Deuteronomy 31:8 (NIV)
"The Lord himself goes before you and will be
with you; he will never leave you nor forsake you.
Do not be afraid; do not be discouraged."

10/11/2008

Here's the latest. Elijah is now in a regular room. (618) They have his shunt completely bypassed now, because he was still having trouble after they pulled the tube out of his belly. His belly is still swelling after he eats, so whatever the problem was before is still there. They are going to let him rest until Monday, and then they will do a CT on his abdomen to see what the problem is with his liver and spleen.

He is still extremely fussy and has not been the Elijah we knew yet. It has taken him a long time to wake up from the surgery, and he still does not have the motor skills he did before. It's almost like he is half asleep, and this, of course, has the doctors somewhat worried. I think the seizures the other night affected his brain again, but the doctors are saying that it wasn't a seizure. They say it was just because of the pressure in his brain. Well, it doesn't matter what you call it, it's still a bad thing.

Anyway, he is eating some, but mostly fussing with a little nap here and there. Hopefully he will get better, especially after they figure out what is going on with his liver and spleen. We don't yet know how long he will be in the hospital, and I guess that would depend on what is wrong with him.

If Paige's mother dies in the meantime, we might need a few folks to help with him, because someone always has to be there. She was talking a little this morning, but I think she is no better.

Well, that's all I have tonight. I'll see you all tomorrow.

Matt

I remember writing this update. I knew Elijah's condition was serious, but I didn't realize how bad it really was just yet. More time was needed before that came into focus. As I look back now, more than 10 years later, I think the greatest thing that sticks out is that I didn't just give up this time. I remember the love I felt for him and how it didn't matter if he ever fully regained what he used to be. I see the evidence of that unconditional love and an example of the father I had always wanted to be. No, I wasn't on top of a pit box at a racetrack, coaching third base at a Little League game, or cheering from the fifty-yard line. I was simply being the dad God had called me to be. Today that means more than anyone who will read this can imagine.

I am also reminded of how turbulent this time was and how it felt like our life as a family was spinning out of control. Donna was dying, Elijah is sick, and our close family was spread out, thin, and vulnerable. We had no answers yet, and it didn't appear that any were coming soon. The only truly tangible things we had were each other and faith. I remember going to bed that night praying for a miracle but willing to accept whatever God had planned. I never imagined just how hard that second part would be.

Oct 13, 2008

Alright, here's the latest. They did his CT today, and it was normal. So, while we praise the Lord that it was normal, we still are right back where we started....we don't know what's wrong. The neurosurgeon and the GI doctor are supposed to come talk to Paige tomorrow morning and give her the plan. As far as I know the general plan is this. They are going to put his shunt back in although they are going to have it drain in a different location.

When they do his shunt surgery, they will also do a liver biopsy to see if that will tell them anything; that is if the neurosurgeon will let them do it during the same procedure. If not, then they will do the biopsy during another procedure.

They are going to do a few more tests on him tomorrow. I think one of them is a sweat test, and I'm not sure what the other tests are. His lab work still shows his bilirubin and liver enzyme levels are high, but they are not climbing. They also are not going down either. Paige did say that the whites in his eyes are now yellow. What's all this mean? Who knows?

The GI doctor says that she can monitor him when he comes into the clinic. I guess that means at least one trip a week to Birmingham after he comes home, maybe two. I'll take that if I can get them home. He may get to come home as early as this weekend, but it all depends on when they want to put his new shunt in. Hopefully we'll find that out tomorrow morning when the doctors come around.

I hope everyone was at church last night, but if you weren't, I'll tell you that it was a blessing. If you were there you know what I mean. Only God knows how much it means to me to have a church family and friends who love the Lord and tolerate me. My feeble words could never express the feelings I have knowing that I have friends that love my family and care about them. Thank you. I am humbled by your love.

Matt

I guess I should explain here what an external shunt is. A shunt is nothing more than a pressure valve for the fluid in your brain. The body normally takes care of this on its own, but because of Elijah's brain bleed, the blood had clotted the two small holes at the base of his brain that allows this fluid to drain. So, a shunt was installed. When that malfunctions, sometimes an external shunt is temporarily put in place. This shunt is nothing more than a tube coming out of your body, draining brain fluid out. How is this regulated since there isn't a pressure valve? It is regulated by keeping an IV-type bag at the same height as the patient's brain. There were other little nuances about it, and I'm sure any medical professional reading this is rolling their eyes. But if you think about holding a water hose up on either end, you know that the water inside will find its way to level. Same principle here. Confused? Yes, I was too. Maybe the best thing for you to know is that while Elijah was this way, he and Paige were bedridden. It was an operation of at least three nurses to move them from the bed. Add that to this already crazy situation, and you'll understand the context of desperation that was clouding my writing at the time.

With that out of the way, I'll tell you about the events at church I mentioned. That Sunday night, October 12th, I was called down front by our pastor. They placed a chair for me in front of the pulpit and asked the church to gather around and lay hands on me. Brother Gary began in prayer, and others followed, asking for healing, peace, comfort, etc. I cannot begin to tell you the feelings that ran through me. Tears ran freely, and the love of God was felt by all there. But the most important thing was that I knew I wasn't alone. Once again, my church had my family's back. They were as invested in my son as much as I was. They loved us well that night, and without knowing, provided much-needed strength for the long journey ahead.

Oct 14, 2008

Well, I just got in from Birmingham, so here's the news. The neurosurgeon came in and said that his white count was extremely high, so he has another or the same infection somewhere. They are starting him on an antibiotic to try and clear that up. He will not do his shunt surgery until that is cleared up, so it will likely be next week before that happens with a slight chance of it happening this week. Elijah did not want to eat today. He ate this morning at 7, and Paige had to force him to eat again at 4 this afternoon. He is still a little fussy, but mostly when he hears someone strange in the room or when the door opens. I guess he's like most kids there and has figured out that when someone comes in it is usually followed by a needle of some sort. We did get him to smile and laugh a little today, so I was encouraged about that.

Also, the doctor said that they will do a liver biopsy whenever they are able to do his shunt surgery. That is all I have for tonight on him.

Paige's mom is about the same, maybe a little better mentally. Maddie wanted to go see her, so I was not going to deny her. It's funny how kids are. Maddie doesn't care how her Maw Maw is. She just wants to cuddle up beside her and talk, and that's just what she did tonight. I didn't rush her for obvious reasons. I was happy that Donna knew she was there and was excited to see her.

Again, thank all of you for your prayers. We'll see you tomorrow.

Matt

I can remember this night well. I left the hospital that evening exhausted and ready to be home. The hospital is 90 miles from our home, and by the time we left, it was pushing 8 pm. That meant it would be 9:30 before Maddie and I made it home, and I still had to give her a bath, get my bath, and get us both fed and in bed. As we left the parking garage, my usual shy and quiet daughter leaned over to me and asked if she could go see Donna. At first, I wanted to say no, but something in me prompted me to turn the truck in the opposite direction.

We arrived at my in-laws' house a little before 8:30. I took Maddie by the hand, and we went into the house and back to Donna's room. To my surprise, Donna was awake and alert. Her faced beamed at the sight of Maddie, and Maddie returned the favor with a smile of her own. Maddie didn't care about Donna's colostomy bag, her hospital bed, or Donna's condition. She just wanted to see her Maw Maw and talk awhile. Once the sight of those two met my eyes, I had to excuse myself for a minute. I went into the kitchen and broke down. After a few minutes of prayer and getting myself together, I returned to Donna's room to find the two of them laying together and talking. We stayed until 10 pm that night, allowing the two of them to fall asleep together before starting the long drive home. I pulled away from their house that night, worried not about the time on the clock but about how much time we had left.

Oct 15, 2008

I know the last email I sent said that the liver biopsy would not happen until the shunt surgery, but the GI doctor wants to do it tomorrow. I do not know a time yet, but I will let everyone know as soon as I do. There is no need for anyone to go (April, Jill, Tiana, Amy, Christy are you listening?), but I did want everyone to know how to pray.

Matt

It felt like I was always trying to keep people from driving an hour and a half to see my son and wife. Why? I don't know. Maybe I didn't want to use up everyone's energy until it was really needed. Maybe it was simple pride. I can't remember. I do recall thinking that we were finally gaining some traction in finding out what was really ailing Elijah. By this time, he and Paige had been in there for a week, and we still had no answers as to why he was so sick.

Oct 16, 2008

Everyone,

Ok, here is the latest. They did the Biopsy today, and they also put in a pic line. The pic line will enable them to draw blood or administer any medicine without the constant IV's or blood draws.

They sent his piece of liver to the Mayo clinic, so we won't know those test results until tomorrow or next week. I'll make sure and send out an email as soon as I know something. The GI doctor did say that she thought that he would need a liver transplant. The piece that she took out was white and hard, so that's why she <u>thinks</u> that is what will need to happen. I underlined the think there, because we will not know anything for sure until the biopsy comes back and the doctor tells us more. I'm sure she knows her practice, but I also know my Lord. His will is going to be done, and it will be perfect. No matter what happens from here on out I will give Him the glory and the honor. I have tried to be careful to do that ever since he was born, and I'm not going to stop now.

With that said, I would appreciate all your prayers, especially for Paige. She is extremely strong, but she was very upset today for obvious reasons. She has a lot on her plate right now, and she needs all the strength God can give her. Outside of God she is the joy of my life. I love her, and my heart breaks for her. I can tell you that without her my faith would not be what it is today.

Well, that's all I have right now. There is a little bit of good news. His white count went down today, and if it continues to go down, they may put his shunt back in next week. As soon as they do that, he will be able to go home. The GI doctor said that she could treat him in the clinic, so he will not have to stay in the hospital for that.

Matt

I think you can tell that the signs were telling us that this was not going to be short nor simple. The words "no matter what happens from here on out" say as much. Once the GI doctor told us the news about his liver, I think both Paige and I knew that life would never be the same as it once was. I tried to convey a message of hope, but I'm not sure I was buying it myself. Paige's desperation that day left me with feelings I am inadequate to describe. I can only say that it felt like we were being swallowed up by a tremendous black hole.

Oct 18, 2008

Everyone,

Ok, I have a lot of information today, so hang on. The GI doctor came around again this morning, and I asked her a lot of questions. Here is the jest of what she said. He does have portal hypertension which means that the blood flow to the liver is somehow blocked. Originally, they were thinking this was due to the IV's that he had in what was left of his umbilical cord shortly after he was born. They are now thinking that it is because his liver was damaged shortly before or after his birth. This causes blood and fluids to back up in his abdomen which has been causing his belly to swell. The part of the liver biopsy that has come back shows that there is an infection in his liver. The antibiotics are clearing that up, and she is going to keep him on them for a couple of more weeks. This does not mean that he will have to stay in the hospital that long, but he will have to keep his pic line in so that we can administer the medicine at home.

The other stains from the biopsy have not come back yet, and they will tell us more about the problems he is having. The labs that they have sent off to other hospitals have not come back. They will show if his problem is just with his liver or other organs as well. This part is very important in determining if he will be a candidate for a liver transplant. If the problems he has also have affected other organs then they will not do a transplant on him. If the problems are only with his liver, then they will. He would be put on the pediatric list waiting for an organ which is usually shorter than the standard adult list. One of us could also be a donor if we are a match, but they do not like to do that here. The good news is that his liver is still functioning, and she expects that we are still a year away from a possible transplant. They will not put his name on a list until they determine if the problems are only with his liver. Pray that it is.

Also, the neurology folks came by. It was only a resident, so he did not know when they were going to do his shunt surgery. I hope we find out Monday. I know this is a lot of information, but hopefully you can make some sense out of it. Please know that Paige and I appreciate your prayers. All of you are a blessing.

Matt

I remember feeling like we had wrapped our heads around the news we had received the day before. There seemed to be a little hope in what we heard, so we latched on to that and asked folks to pray with us. All we could do at this point was trust God.

Oct 21, 2008

Everyone,

Well, here is the latest. The GI doctor said that his white count has not come down the past two days, so his shunt surgery has been put on hold. I guess that takes away the likelihood of them getting back home this week. He will be on antibiotics until Friday, but she says that they apparently are having no effect on whatever is keeping his count up. That may be the least of our worries at this point.

The doctor (different GI doctor from last week) said that they might not approve Elijah for a liver transplant because of his developmental delays. We could give him part of ours, and if the rest of the tests that we are waiting on come back positive then that's what will happen. I'll give him all of mine if I must. Still no word on when we'll see those results.

Also, in other bad news, his belly is still swollen, and they are going to do a chest x-ray to see why. The medicine they've been giving him has been working, but not as fast or as well as they would like. I guess there's something going on there too.

There is a little good news. He slept most of the night last night which allowed Paige to get some rest. Maddie and I are going up this afternoon, and again Friday-Saturday. We'll also go up whenever they do his surgery if by some miracle it is this week.

Thank you for your prayers and thank all of you who have asked me about them. It is never a bother for me to give anyone an update. It is better to have a bathroom trip in church take 15 minutes because of giving updates than for no one to ask about him at all. I know you are praying, and I know that you care about my family.

By this all men will know that you are my disciples, if you love one another." John 13:35 (NIV)

Thank you,

Matt

I remember how mad Paige was when we were told that he might not be an organ transplant candidate because of his developmental problems. I think the lady had bad information, but at the time, it was gospel truth to us. During this time, as doctors tried to sort things out, it felt as if we were going nowhere and that my family would never be at home again. There seemed to be no end in sight, and God had yet to show up and show off. We desperately needed a miracle only he could provide. I longed for any hint of normalcy.

Oct 22, 2008

Everyone,

Maddie and I went to the hospital last night and spent a few hours with Eli and Paige. He was in a pretty good mood. I did get him to smile and laugh a little bit. His skin is turning yellow, but I guess that's to be expected with his liver problems.

Still no word on any of the other blood tests that they ran last week. I did get to speak to the neurosurgeon resident, so I asked about their plans for his shunt. Of course, they want to wait until his white count comes down to normal, but it has stopped dropping even with the two weeks on a couple of antibiotics.

Paige said the GI doctor came in this morning and said that his blood sugar level was all messed up too. She asked the doctor what the plan was, and all she would say is that she and the neurosurgeon were going to be back later today to discuss what they were going to do. I had hoped we could get his shunt back in this week, and maybe get them home by next week. But it's looking like they are finding out more things to keep him for every day. I guess we're back to one day at a time again.

Well, that's all I have for now. If I hear something from Paige, I'll be sure and send another email out. Also, I'm putting these on caringbridge.org. The site name is elijahpartain. Thank you, April, for setting that up.

Ya'll be good,

Matt

Unless you've had your child in the hospital this long, you can't appreciate how hard it is. Countless hours waiting on doctors who themselves are waiting on tests. More tests, blood draws, and needle sticks, which means more crying and impatience. Added to that is the fact that he still has an external shunt. Paige has been bedridden with him for two weeks at this point. The situation grew more dire by the day, and the storm clouds grew ever darker.

Oct 22, 2008

Everyone,

Just heard from Paige, and he is having shunt surgery tomorrow. They are going to be putting the drain from his shunt into his vascular system with the end of the drain near his heart. This is a little riskier than the other way, but it's all they can do now. The doctor is ok doing the surgery even though his white count is not normal. He said that if it's not going up, we're ok.

She has not heard from the GI doctor again today, so there might be yet another update a little later. I'm not going to hold my breath, but I'm hoping we can get them home this weekend. It's only been 4 weeks.

That's all for now. Thank you for your prayers, and your cards. Every one of you are a blessing.

Matt

I remember the feeling I had when I wrote this. I thought I would finally have my family back together under one roof before much longer. There was actually a little hope, a small ray that penetrated the darkness. I took the afternoon off from work, asked my dad to come down, and cleaned the house a little better than I had before. I didn't want Paige to come home to anything other than a spotless home. Dad could take care of Maddie because I had to help cook supper at church that night.

Each Wednesday night, our church has a fellowship supper that starts at 5:15. Different groups within the church prepare the meal from week to week. Although the cost for those eating is minimal, it helps raise money for the groups doing the cooking.

Since I am the drummer for the Praise Band, I helped cook on the Wednesdays we were scheduled for. Our specialty as a group is breakfast, and Jonathan Stuart and I cooked the pancakes. The two of us had been doing this together for years, and we had it down to a science. It's something I wouldn't skip, even as my family was separated, because it brought back some sense of normalcy. If nothing else, it allowed my mind some time to relax. That evening, as I walked through the doors of the Fellowship Hall, apron in hand, my heart and pride took a massive hit.

The first thing I noticed as I walked through the doors was the table where the money is collected. My eyes were drawn to that, as they usually are, and they were met with a sign that read,

"All of tonight's proceeds will go towards Eli Partain's medical bills."

I stopped in my tracks. I'm sure the look on my face betrayed my mind because Randy Godfrey came running from the kitchen toward me, saying, "No. No. You let us do this! This is how we love! This is how God uses His people to answer prayers. You let us do this!"

My head dropped as tears fell from my eyes. Randy embraced me, just as he had done the day Elijah was born, and consoled me as the waves of emotion washed over my soul. What do you say in the face of such generosity? How could I face these people? Somehow, they had found out about our financial struggles and had done what the people of God are commanded to do; they loved my family and me.

Randy led me out into the hallway, and I gathered my emotions back into check. After asking if I was alright, he prayed over me again, and afterward, we walked back into the kitchen together. I didn't feel alone anymore. I felt those around me leaning in and helping me with a burden I couldn't bear. I'm not sure I could ever put words onto paper to help someone understand how profound that statement is, but to know you are loved by your brothers and sisters in Christ is beyond powerful; it is supernatural.

After cooking supper that night and practicing Sunday's service afterward, I called Paige. There were tears on both ends of the call, and even though we were in the middle of a nightmare, there was joy in the moment. Folks, that's all God.

Oct 23, 2008

Everyone,

Well, a 9:30 surgery turned into a 1:30 surgery, and he was just brought out from recovery. The doctor said that everything went extremely smooth, but of course we won't know if "the surgery is good until the baby is good." Praise the Lord for a successful surgery! Hopefully this is just one obstacle down with a few more to go.

Still no word on any of the other blood work from last week, but it will be a few weeks before any of that comes back. They told us this morning that his liver biopsy is being looked at by some other doctors, because no one is sure what it really is right now. I am confident that the Lord knows what it is, and He will take care of the rest of it.

Thank every one of you for your prayers. Also, thank you to my church family. You are a blessing to us. I have no words (no comment here, Randy Godfrey) to tell you how much you all mean to me. A simple thank you could never be enough, but for now I guess it will have to do.

I love y'all,

Matt

We were perturbed by a late surgery, but that turned into joy when Paige could finally get up and walk around the room and hospital floor with Elijah. She was finally on her feet again, and there was at least a little joy in that small step forward. I was still dumbfounded by the generosity and love shown by our church, and I couldn't thank God enough for answering our prayers.

That evening, after the surgery, Maddie went home with my parents to stay the night, as I drove home alone with my thoughts and prayers. I hoped Paige and Elijah would be coming home soon. It seemed like forever since anything felt normal, and I longed for the comfort that is felt when all of our voices echo off of the dark brown logs of our home. It was a form of soothing music to my ears; the sounds of a home that is alive with the giggles of a little girl and the laughter of a special son. This night there wouldn't be any of that God-given music. All that resonated against those logs were the sounds of a lonely man praying desperately for what his mind and heart longed for: a healed son.

Oct 24, 2008

Everyone,

I just heard from Paige, and Elijah will be having surgery again today. The drain that goes into his heart is not in the right place, so they will have to cut him in both places again to fix it. The neurosurgeon said that this will not affect the timeframe of getting him home. We are waiting on the GI folks for that. I think he may get to come home Monday if they can get everything lined up with home health care, and if this surgery is successful.

Also, the GI doctor said yesterday that she was going to check again on his liver biopsy today to see what the other doctors thought was wrong.

That's all I have for now, and I will update again after the surgery. Thank you for your prayers.

Be good if you can, I can't,

Matt

The prospect of getting them home made me happy as I wrote this. I felt like we were crossing one item off of our list and only had a couple of more to go. If you couldn't tell, I was more than ready for them to be home. Home meant normal, and nothing about them being 90 miles away from me seemed normal. I was ready for it to be over and for my family to be whole again.

Oct 24, 2008

Everyone,

Well, he is out of surgery, and you're not going to believe this. The surgery went well, and the doctor said that it was a good thing that the tube was not in the right place. While doing the surgery, they found a tear and a kink right below the valve in the line they put in yesterday. This was causing the fluid to leak under his skin. Not to mention that if the kink had not been there, then he would have had an open tear in the tube that is going into his heart with nothing to stop blood from escaping out. I'm not a doctor, and I didn't stay at a Holiday Inn Express last night, but I don't think that would be a good thing. Praise the Lord for another surgery, and for showing the doctors what was wrong.

Again, thank all of you for praying. I know that the

prayer of the righteous is powerful and effective......and so does Elijah.

Matt

A little setback, but I was thankful for the little things that God does without us knowing.

Oct 24, 2008

Ok, this hopefully will be the last update for today. The GI doctors came by and said that he has cirrhosis of the liver. He has some liver tissue that is working, but not much. They still don't know what has caused this. It could've happened after he was born, or it could be a metabolic issue. The lab work that has been sent off will tell us if it is metabolic or not.

Also, his newest X-ray shows that everything about today's surgery went well. Everything is in the right place, and his shunt should be ok. They are thinking he will get to come home next Tuesday. We have to wait and see what his blood sugar levels do. He may have to have a tube to be fed with if they cannot get his levels right. After he gets to come home Paige will still have to take him to the hospital at least once a week to see the doctor in clinic. I would imagine it will be in these appointments when we find out if they will do a liver transplant. As soon as I know when they are I will let you know, so that we can bathe them in prayer.

Thank you everyone for your words of encouragement, and for your prayers.

Matt

Everything seemed to be going in the right direction.

We were getting a few answers, and the thought of going home was going to be a reality very soon. If he were able to come home, our thoughts were that Paige could stay at her parent's house for a while so that she could be close to the hospital and she could help with her mother.

Looking back, I think that hurt her about as much as anything; to know your Mother is dying and you're unable to help in any way because your son is so sick. As much as I felt my world was falling apart, it couldn't compare to what Paige was going through. To her credit, she stayed strong and held her ground. I never once saw her lose the grace she has always walked with. I don't know how else to word that, but if you've ever seen it, you know what I mean. It's what attracted me to her all those years ago, and I believe it is the foundation for her timeless beauty.

After the surgery, my parents came to my house with Maddie. I asked them to stay the night, to which they agreed, because I wanted to go back to Birmingham the next day to see Paige and Eli again. Maybe I could take care of Elijah for the day, and Paige could go see her Mother.

Oct 25, 2008

Everyone,

I came up this morning to see them, and he is doing ok. His belly is really swollen, and they are going to give him some medicine to hopefully get it back down. His blood sugars are still dropping during the night, and if they do again tonight they will put in an NG tube. The doctor said that it might have been doing that before, but they can't ignore it once they find it.

Also, she said that the doctors believe this is a metabolic problem. I asked her about it so that I could get my facts straight, and I would know what we could be up against. She said that a metabolic problem means that his body has a problem with the way he metabolizes certain things. Those things deposit in the liver and damage the tissue. Putting in a new liver wouldn't do anything with a problem like this except damage another liver. Certain metabolic problems can be treated, but only a hand full at this time. If this is a metabolic problem, then we'll pray for the treatable ones. If it is a metabolic problem, and it is a treatable one, then they may put his name on a transplant list. Of course, Paige and I could be donors, but we're getting way ahead of ourselves already. We'll just pray for something treatable, and for the Lord's will. His will is perfect, and I know that He loves Elijah more than I ever could. He gave up His son for him. I wouldn't give up my son for anyone.

Matt

At this point, I knew that the odds of Elijah having a long life were slim. I had often thought of how we would take care of him after we were gone, but now those thoughts shifted to giving him quality of life instead of quantity. I worried about insurance issues; we were already seeing bills come to us because of the coverage we had. I tried my best to keep that from Paige. She had enough on her plate.

In the meantime, I kept praying for a miracle. God could do anything, I reasoned, so I wore out my prayer time with everything Elijah. In doing that, a funny thing happened. It seemed the more I prayed, the closer I became to God, and the more I trusted Him with Elijah. I realized that Elijah was more His than mine, and I trusted Him to be the perfect Father only He could be. As my son struggled, I found comfort at the feet of Jesus. With every little bit of bad news we received, I prayed. When we received good news, I praised in prayer. I made a habit of praying my way home from the hospital. I would try to go up to Birmingham every other day, and I spent the hour and a half on the way back praying as Maddie slept.

This time of my life would teach me more about the power of prayer than in any other phase of my life before. It's a power I wouldn't easily forget and one that God knew I would need in the future.

Oct 26, 2008

Everyone,

Well, Paige just called, and he's going back to surgery today as soon as they can get the OR ready. His shunt is apparently leaking in the same place as the other day. They are removing the shunt, and putting the liquid loop back in. So, we are right back where we were last week. It's very disappointing to say the least. It seems as though we will never get them home.

Before this his belly was still swollen, and they are now thinking that it is not fluid. It is most likely that his organs are swollen because of the problems with his liver. I did not hear about the blood sugar count, but at this point it really doesn't matter. We'll get them home in the Lord's time. I'll let ya'll know something later tonight.

Matt

Talk about a gut punch! I remember the feeling I had when Paige called me, and that's about the only way I can describe it. I had a hard time praying that night, but I did anyway. My prayer time beside my bed was spent lifting Paige up. I heard the disappointment in her voice, and I felt the desperation through the phone, so I asked God to help her however He could. I didn't even know what to ask God to do. I left it in His hands, and I wondered how we'd ever make it through this dark time.

Oct 26, 2008

Everyone,

The surgery went well, and he is back to having the external shunt. This means that he and Paige are basically confined to a bed or chair, and that really doesn't suit either one of them. The reason they didn't put in another shunt is because they need to check for infection. Paige said the doctor didn't understand why this one had a leak in the tube, and that it may have been a defect from the factory. Whatever it is has cost them another week in the hospital at the least. There is no time plan for getting his next shunt in. I hope they tell us tomorrow.

Maddie and I will be going up tomorrow, and again on Thursday. If they're still in there Saturday, we'll be celebrating Maddie's birthday there. I'll update again tomorrow after the doctors' round.

Matt

I was mad, but I didn't know at who. Our lives were upside down, and someone was to blame; I just didn't know where to place all that I felt. I prayed, but to be honest, it seemed my prayers were falling to the ground. I was desperate, and I longed for normalcy. I tried my best to keep Paige's spirits up, but looking back, I think we simply held on to each other. Like a couple of people lost at sea, we held on to the only lifeboat of hope we had: Jesus. I remember how hard it was to trust Him, but at this point, what other choice did we have?

Oct 27, 2008

Everyone,

I just spoke with Paige, and Elijah is in renal failure (kidney). They think this was caused by one of two things. It was most likely all the antibiotics that he has been on, but it also could be related to the fact that he has been to the OR 5 times in 3 days. They are going to start treating him for this, but he cannot have his shunt put back in until this is resolved. The renal doctor team will be coming by to look at him later on today, so hopefully we'll know more then.

Also, they may have to start drawing fluid from his belly if the medicine they are giving him continues not to work. He had an ultrasound this morning to determine if the problems with his belly swelling is fluid or if his organs are swelling. They were thinking it was his spleen yesterday, but I think this renal failure has caused them to take another look at it just being fluid.

That's all I have for now. I will update everyone when I hear from them again, or after Maddie and I get up there this evening.

Thank you again for your many prayers.

Matt

Oct 27, 2008

I just spoke with Paige, and the genetics/metabolic and renal doctors have rounded. The genetic folks want a bunch of lab work to determine what has happened to his liver. I think that was the lab work that was supposed to have been taken this morning. They didn't say when they were going to do it. They also want a piece of his muscle tissue whenever they do the next surgery, so they can check for other diseases.

The renal doctor has given us two possibilities as to what is wrong with his kidneys. 1: The antibiotics have caused damage to his kidneys. This can be reversed, although he didn't say how. 2: He is not getting blood flow to his kidneys because of his liver failure. This cannot be reversed and would require dialysis at some point. But, it would not correct the problem, and would only be something to give us a little more time before his other organs are affected.

Maddie and I are on our way up there, so there might be another update tonight. Still no word on the ultrasound that they did this morning. Please keep praying,

Matt

Another day, and more problems. It seemed as if bad news were all the doctors could tell us. I wondered how this would end. Would God work a miracle? Would He intervene in such a way that only He could get the glory for it? I hoped so, and I prayed for as much, but He had a mess to work with here. I prayed hard that night after Maddie and I got home. I felt like God would eventually answer, but I wasn't sure how. All I could do was trust Him even when I couldn't see anything that resembled Him in what was going on.

CHAPTER 12

THE MONSTER AT THE DOOR

Psalm 38:9 (NIV)
"All my longings lie open before you, Lord; my sighing is not hidden from you."

Oct 28, 2008

Everyone,

I just talked with Paige, and the news is not good. The GI doctor came in and said that the medicine they gave him yesterday for his kidneys did not work. They are going to give it to him again today to see if maybe it will help. So, with his liver and kidneys both failing they have given us one of two options. 1: We can stop where we are right now. 2: We can start him on dialysis and wait for his liver to completely fail. He will not be a candidate for a liver transplant since his kidneys are now failing too.

Maddie and I will be heading up there again in a few minutes, because I need to be with Paige. Please be in prayer for her. She is having a lot put on her shoulders with this and her mother. But, God's grace is enough...It is sufficient, and I know that this will glorify Him. Thank you for your prayers.

Matt

I felt gutted again. The doctor that Paige had talked to actually said the word we had feared since all of this started; "terminal." According to him, our little boy was not going to get better. He was going to die slowly and painfully in front of our eyes. I couldn't type the word *terminal* in that update. I couldn't. My mind couldn't seem to accept that fact. I prayed recklessly through tears as I drove up the interstate that day. What could I say? What could I possibly say to my beautiful wife? To Maddie? To all that were praying for a miracle that wouldn't happen? How could I explain God's love to anyone ever again? What I felt wasn't love. Then, my phone rang. It was Charleen Gore, Brother Larry's wife.

Mrs. Charleen is a wonderful lady who had ministered to us, especially Paige, through some of our most difficult days, this one included. I knew that she and a few others were planning a trip to see Paige and Elijah but weren't sure when. Would you believe that they were there when the doctor gave Paige the news? Would you believe that this story gets better than that? Let me take you back a few months. It'll change the way this story looks, and it'll show you, as it did me that day, how God has everything in His hands.

In the spring and fall of each year, our church offers "Growth Groups" on Sunday and Wednesday nights. Paige and I usually participate in one of these groups, most of which follow along in a Christian book or Bible study. In the spring of 2008, Paige took part in a lady's study that Mrs. Charleen led. Over a few months, the members of that group grew close to each other, although I was sure Paige had been her usual quiet and reserved self and remained distant from everyone in there except for Christy Stuart. The day after the last session, I received a call from Mrs. Charleen, and she asked if Paige had told me what happened in their class the evening before. I told her that she hadn't, and as she tried to speak again, she broke down into tears.

She said that Paige had not spoken one word during the many nights the ladies were together. Everyone had shared something, at one time or another, except for her. About midway through this study, one of the other ladies, Carol Coram, had approached Mrs. Charleen about Paige and told her that she was burdened to pray for Paige. She knew something wasn't right. To Mrs. Coram's credit, she was on to something.

The last night of the study started the same as the others, but Mrs. Charleen opened the floor up for anyone to talk about how they were impacted by the book they had gone through. Person after person spoke as Paige sat still until Mrs. Charleen was about ready to close the group. Suddenly, Paige burst out into tears and raised her shaky voice.

She finally mustered the words to say what was on her heart. As she spoke, she talked of doubting God, learning to accept His will, and as she did, she began to release her spirit from the cage she had built. During this scene, Mrs. Coram began praising God aloud, her hands lifted in the air. Ladies gathered around Paige, praying and ministering to her, as the Holy Spirit guided each one.

As Mrs. Charleen described that scene to me, I broke down into tears myself. At that moment, she thought she had lost control of the group, something I wouldn't argue about because God himself had taken it over.

During this chaotic scene, as Paige was finally releasing years of emotions, these women became more than a simple growth group. These ladies became something of a ministry to my wife and would help my family through one of the most difficult days of our lives. I liked to refer to them as the "hen house" because wherever they gathered, it sounded much like a gaggle of hens. It was a term of endearment, and I can't thank these ladies enough for the way they have loved Paige through the years.

It had been about an hour since I talked to Paige when I answered Mrs. Charleen's call. She asked me if I knew they were there, and, after telling her I didn't, she began to recall what had happened during their visit.

Six of the ladies from the "hen house" were able to find time to make the trip to Birmingham that day to see Paige and Elijah. They rode together that morning, and as they talked, one of them mentioned that they believed that God had a plan and a purpose for them on *this* day. They weren't sure what it was, but the gentle whisper and leading of the Holy Spirit had guided them to the hospital at this appointed time. From what I understand, there was an air of expectancy in April Sexton's van as they traveled the 90 or so miles to see Paige and Elijah.

Once there, the ladies took turns holding Elijah, and it was Brandy Ryals who had him in her arms when the doctor came in to talk with Paige. A few moments earlier, Elijah had begun to get fussy, so Brandy began to sing to him his song, *Jesus Loves Me*. About the time he calmed back down, the doctor's words of a terminal diagnosis were finding Paige's ears. As Paige broke down, the other ladies began to pray over her while Brandy continued serenading my son. Indeed, Brandy's simple children's song would be the soundtrack of God's faithfulness in our worst moment of this arduous journey thus far.

Let me write that again, in another way, so that you will understand. Paige had the one group of ladies she trusted, women who had ministered to her and loved her well, surrounding her as she received the news no mother ever wants to hear.

Brandy recalled her experience with Elijah to me, and it is one that still brings tears to my eyes today. She rocked my boy, sang to him, and did her best to comfort him as his mother was finding out our time with him was limited. I can't think about that day without being in awe of God. Yes, on the day I found out my son's illness was terminal, I praised God for His love for us. Brandy didn't know it, but that simple children's song she sang became an anthem for me that day. I knew Jesus loved me because why else would He have provided those ladies to Paige, and Mrs. Charleen's phone call to me? Yes, Jesus loves me; I know that He loves me, because the Bible tells me so. The part of that song that would become a struggle is at the end. *"Little ones to Him belong, they are weak, but He is strong."*

After I had hung up with Mrs. Charleen, I began to digest all of the information she had given me. There was more to it than what Paige had been able to explain through her brokenness and tears. The message from the doctor couldn't have been worse, but there was a supernatural peace from God at the moment.

Once arriving at the hospital, I ran up to Elijah's room with Maddie in my arms. There I found Mrs. Charleen waiting on me outside of the hospital room. The ladies were still there, not wanting to leave Paige by herself.

After the ladies left, the room was once again quiet and still. I looked at my beautiful yet tired wife, and our eyes met. I slowly walked over to Paige and Elijah and placed my hand on my son's head. Neither of us spoke as I caressed his back. We didn't have to. We just looked at each other through tear-laden eyes. There weren't words for this moment. It was almost as if our souls communicated to each other through our gaze. I can't tell you how long that lasted, but afterward, I held him and began to silently recall in my mind all that God had brought us through. I stayed later than I usually did; rest wouldn't come that night anyway. In truth, a real rest wouldn't come again for longer than anyone would have imagined.

As I got home later that night, I felt the need to update the page. I knew word about his terminal prognosis had gotten out by now, and I felt like I needed to address the people who were faithfully praying for my family.

Oct 28, 2008

Everyone,

Maddie and I just got home, so I thought I would send out a big thank you to everyone for your prayers. The neurosurgeon came in and said that they would not do his shunt until next week. The GI doctor never came back around, so that I could ask her a few more questions especially about the time that we have. They tried to put an NG (feeding tube through his nose) tube in, but he kept gagging it up into his mouth, so they stopped trying. They'll just put him on some IV fluids if his blood sugar goes back down again tonight.

I guess the main question everyone has right now is what we are going to do. First, we are going to praise the Lord. He is our strength. Then, we're going to pray and ask Him for guidance. That's all we can do.

I want to tell everyone who called, prayed, and those who stopped by today (especially the Hen House) a big thank you. We are extremely blessed. God has worked everything out ahead of time, and sometimes it's just plain cool to see it come together. Even in a time like this. I'll update tomorrow as soon as we hear something from the GI doctors.

Matt

That update would have read a lot different if it weren't for God's provision and grace. I can't say any more about it. It's hard to come up with words when you learn that the time you have left with your son is very short. Even now, a little over ten years later, it's hard to write as I relive that day.

Oct 29, 2008

Everyone,

OK, the GI doctors finally came by today. Paige asked her what kind of a timeframe we were looking at. She doesn't know. The renal doctors have not been by yet, and she is going to ask them the same question. The plan is now to have his shunt put in next week and to let him come home. The GI folks can monitor his liver through clinic visits once or twice a week, as can the renal doctors with the kidneys. They are still going to treat him with different medicine, but we are not going to start him on dialysis.

They took a lot of lab work today and will take just as much tomorrow. This is the lab work to determine what metabolic problem he has with his liver. They want to make sure that it is not something that is genetic. The renal folks want the lab work to determine just how much kidney function he has.

As far as his physical condition, he is miserable. His belly is swollen even more, and he is having to take short breathes because of the pressure on his lungs. His legs and feet are also swollen, but they are trying to give him medicine to make those come down. The only problem with that is your kidneys do most of the work, even with the medicine.

Maddie and I are not going up today, but we will be up there tomorrow, Friday night, and all day Saturday. Please continue to pray for him. He is strong and courageous. I hope I can be too.

Matt

Even though we were asking about the amount of time we had with our son, we sort of knew that we didn't have long. There aren't words to describe the feelings that you have in this situation. It is somewhere around the intersection of sadness and helplessness. You are given a crash course in how fragile life is, and how you really can't control anything.

The "strong and courageous" phrase came to mind

as I was writing this update, because of how my son endured the endless pricks, sticks, and surgeries, as well as being confined to that bed. Granted, he really had no choice, but it could have been a lot worse. I needed to draw upon that same kind of strength if I was to go through this with my eyes fixed on Jesus while in a situation I had no choice of being in myself.

Also, I think there was one thing that scared me more than losing my son: losing my faith. At this point in our ordeal, I saw a very real path to losing my faith. I was at a crossroads of sorts. As Henry Blackaby says in his course *Experiencing God*, I found myself at a "crisis of belief." What I believed about God and how I led my family was about to take center stage to those watching our lives. I hoped I could be as strong and courageous spiritually as I saw my son being physically. I hoped I could endure with the grace that only God can provide.

That night at our church's Fall Festival, our Children's Minister, Tiana Gann, had a booth selling T-shirts for our son. The sign once again declared that the proceeds would go towards Eli's medical bills. The front of those shirts was adorned with "I love Eli." The word "love" had been traded in for a simple outlined heart, and on the back was the Bible verse Philippians 1:6:

> *"Being confident of this, that he who began a good work in you will carry it on to completion until the day of Christ Jesus."*

I was torn up emotionally again. T-shirts? Really? Would God and His people stop at nothing to love us and answer prayers? Everywhere I looked, through tear-laden eyes, I saw people with my son's name on the front of their shirt. It was humbling. It was overwhelming. What I couldn't have known then was that God's plan for those shirts was greater than just that night. He was already working well into the future, a future that none of us had envisioned.

Oct 30, 2008

Everyone,

I'm sorry for getting this out late today (Cathy Graham), but I just got home from Birmingham. I usually get to use the PC there, but I held Elijah the entire time I was there today. The GI doctors came in today and just reiterated what we already knew. His liver is causing his abdomen to swell with fluids, and even though they are giving him medicine, it is not going down.

His kidney blood work was better today, but only by a tenth of a point. His kidneys are working, just not as well as they should. Although his numbers were better, his stomach grew another inch in circumference. They could draw the fluid out of his abdomen, but as she said, "It will only come back." We asked her to send the renal doctor by tomorrow so that we could get a clearer picture of what we're headed for. She also told us that he is scheduled to have his shunt put back in next Tuesday. Hopefully, that means we can have him home by Thursday or so, but I'm not getting my hopes up just yet. I still don't see how they can do surgery on him with his breathing the way it is, but who knows?

That's all I have for today. Every one of you are a blessing. We have been receiving emails and cards from people we don't know. They are praying for Elijah, and when I think about the lives He is touching through my son, it makes me smile.

"Humble yourselves, therefore, under God's mighty hand, that He may lift you up in due time. Cast all your anxiety on Him because He cares for you." 1 Peter 5: 6-7

Matt

During this time, it wasn't unusual for me to find envelopes on the drum stool before I began playing for each service. Inside was everything from handwritten notes to greeting cards and personal letters. Some contained money to help us with medical bills. That previous sentence is written in nine words, but accepting an anonymous gift takes a humility that even the longest sentence strains to explain.

Often, we'd get cards in the mail, as well as email, from around the country. I still have most of those cards, and from time to time, I'll go back and read them. They offer a testament to the goodness of God and remind me that even in the darkest times, God is at work, and I am not alone.

Oct 31, 2008

Everyone,

Well, as most of you know, Paige's mom took a turn for the worse this morning. Her blood pressure was 60 over 40 after they were finally able to read it. Most of the morning, they were not able to get a good pressure on her. My mom went to the hospital this morning so that Paige could be with her mom. At the moment, she is hanging in there, and the nurse said it could be a couple of more days of this. I have heard where they have called the family in several times before the actual death, so we may have a few more of these.

As far as Elijah goes, we actually have a little good news today. His creatinine level (I hope that's right) came down again today. That is the level that shows the kidney function. It was 1.5 two days ago, 1.4 yesterday, and 1.1 today. Normal is 0.2. The GI doctor came in today, but only Mom was there, so we didn't get to ask any questions about it. The swelling in his legs and feet went down since yesterday, but his belly gained another 1.5 cm. I think I said inches yesterday, but it's measured in cm. He is still taking the short breaths like yesterday, and he is still very uncomfortable. We'll take the good news today. We haven't had any in a while, so it's nice to hear some every now and again. All the lab work is still out, so we still don't know anything yet. For the moment though, his kidneys appear to be getting better. Praise the Lord! Of course, these feelings are mixed because, at this time, they are still saying that his liver problem is metabolic and that is a terminal diagnosis. I'll praise the Lord either way. He is my strength. The renal doctors have not come by today, and we really wanted to ask them a few questions.

That's all I have for today. I'll be up there until Saturday night, so I'll likely have an update tomorrow for you.

Matt

Nothing can prepare you for the loss of your mother. Paige was actively going through that process but couldn't support her mother in the way she wanted. Instead, she was in the hospital with our dying son, and I'm not sure I can ever relate to what she must have felt during this time. I'm not sure I would want to if I could.

This was the day that separated Donna's time on this earth between living and dying. Before this day, even after Hospice was called in, she was still herself. Some days, you wondered if she was under a terminal diagnosis, and other days you knew days like this one were coming. But those days never prepared you for this. This was the ugly part of death, the slow and deliberate part. It was on days like this one that I imagined just how terrible it would be when Elijah reached them. I never let those thoughts linger for long. It hurt too much.

For now, though, Donna was breathing, and her heart was beating. As badly as Paige wanted to be with her, she still found her way back to the hospital, to Elijah, her beloved son. She was, as she had always been, a wonderful, caring mother, just as her mother had been to her.

I stayed that night at my parent's house because we were going right back to the hospital the next day to celebrate Maddie and Elijah's birthdays. We planned a simple party, just something to help an almost 4-year-old girl feel normal, but in truth, I don't know how many of us felt like having a party.

Nov 1, 2008

Everyone,

Well, we've been here all day, and no doctors have come by. I thought I would go ahead and send out an update before Cathy got on my case again. His creatinine level was 0.9 today, so that's good news again. His belly grew another 1.5 cm, so that's bad news. If his kidney levels go back to normal, I would assume that it means his kidneys will be OK. I don't know this for a fact because the renal doctors have not come by in several days. We are going to ask the GI doctors about this whenever they come by today. As far as we know, his shunt surgery is planned for Tuesday, but that is subject to change. If it is, we may get him home for his birthday on Thursday.

Well, that's all I have for now. If anyone comes today, I'll update again. Thank you again for your prayers.

Matt

What was left out of that update is something I chose to keep personal at the time. You know those moments, don't you? The small moments in life that are so precious, you are scared to put them into words because that might somehow diminish them. I will try to put words to an experience that day and somehow not take away from the preciousness of it.

As we walked into the hospital, we were met by our friends, Jonathan and Christy Stuart, and their three children, Grace, Samantha, and Jud. All five were wearing "I love Eli" shirts as well as big smiles on their faces. I was instantly humbled and concerned at the same time.

The humbled part is easy to explain. Not only had they driven 100 miles to see all of us, but they had come bearing gifts and a happy heart. The concern was for what they were about to see. Christy had already made her way to the hospital on a couple of occasions, but this would be the first time her children, all under the age of seven, would see Elijah in his current condition.

By this time, Elijah no longer looked like anyone would have remembered. His belly was extremely swollen, while the rest of him was thin and frail. The numerous machines hooked to him, along with the bandages from his surgeries, made this a scary sight for someone who wasn't prepared. I guess what I'm trying to say is that I was worried that the sight of him might frighten their three young children. But this family wasn't just any other family. They were like a part of our own family and would look at Elijah through the lens of love. But I guess before I get into that, I need to tell you more about this family that has blessed us so much.

***

Jonathan and Christy are a wonderful couple a few years older than Paige and me. He is a firefighter in Montgomery, and she is an Occupational Therapist. We had initially met them at church because he started playing guitar in the Praise Band. Jonathan and I talked some, and before long, our families began eating supper together once or twice a week. By the time 2008 rolled around, we were involved in a band called Elijah's Promise, and we spent a lot of time together. Even though we had only known the Stuart family for a few years, it sure felt like they had always been a part of our lives. During this time, God used them to minister to us in ways that no one else could.

***

As we made our way into Elijah's room, I nervously watched Grace, Samantha, and Jud to gauge their reactions to him. Jud stood quietly beside his mother, looking for reassurance that everything was ok. After looking Elijah over, Samantha started playing with Maddie in the corner of the room, but seven-year-old Grace—I will never forget what she did.

Grace walked over to the side of Elijah's bed with a look on her face that exuded compassion. Her big brown eyes stared at Elijah as she looked him over from head to toe. She raised her hand up, and then placed it gently on Elijah's back, and said, "Get better soon, Eli. We love you. We've been praying for you."

I turned to look out the window, trying to hide my welled eyes. I had been concerned about what these precious children may think when they saw my son in his condition, but to their credit, they saw their friend in need of love and prayer. I'll never forget that moment, the way that Grace looked at him, and the tenderness in which she spoke. There was a love in her voice that this world could use a lot more of.

After a while, we sang Happy Birthday to Maddie and cut a cake. It wasn't the grand celebration we had a year earlier, but it was the best we could do under the circumstances.

On the day before Maddie turned four, we were trying to make the day as happy as we could for her. That evening, as she and I left the hospital for the long drive home, I asked her if she had enjoyed her day. She replied with a simple smile and then laid her head on the pillow I kept between us. Before we exited the parking deck, she was already fast asleep, on her last day of being three.

Nov 3, 2008
Everyone,

I'm sorry I didn't get an update out yesterday, but there's really nothing new. His creatinine level dropped again yesterday, although I don't know by how much. They have had him on morphine since Friday, and it has let him (and Paige) finally get some rest. She said that they may have to go up on it again today, because he didn't sleep last night at all. A pain management team is supposed to come by and see him sometime. I think they will decide how we are to treat his pain when he goes home. So far, only the neurosurgery folks have been by today, and Paige said that the doctor wants a different surgeon to do his next surgery. He is a specialist in the type of shunt that they will be putting in. Hopefully, this will take place tomorrow, but we don't know yet.

The GI people have not been by, and I think she has some questions for them. His belly is still the same, but I don't know if they have measured it today or not. I will update a little later after she hears some more information.

Paige's sister kept Elijah yesterday so that Paige could go see her Mom. She is still hanging on. Her breathing is getting shallower by the day, and she started having seizures yesterday. Paige said she was very stiff, and of course, she does not know anything. I talked to Randy (Paige's Dad), and he said that they could not find a pulse this morning but that she is still breathing. By everyone's guess, it will likely be today or tomorrow. We appreciate your prayers and concern. I cannot begin to tell you what they mean to us.

Matt

At this point, we were numb to all that was going on around us. Our lives were filled with death and sickness instead of life and health. All that we may have taken for granted at one time was replaced by all that we had feared. We walked, almost as zombies, through the days that felt as if they would never end. In truth, we likely wished they wouldn't because our loved ones were still with us. But that would be a selfish prayer.

By this time, we were praying for God's mercy with Donna, and I wondered, once again, what this would look like with my son. I prayed that I would never know the answer to that. But even in that prayer, my heart was heavy with grief and pain. There was a feeling of impending sorrow, a black cloud, if you will, hanging over us, and we were all powerless to change it.

Nov 3, 2008

Everyone,

I just spoke with Paige, and the GI doctor and pain management team just came by. The GI doctor is new because they work on two-week shifts. If he were to be there another two weeks, he would have yet another GI doctor, but we're hoping that won't happen. This guy wants to try him on some more aggressive medicine to try and get his belly back down. He has been on this medicine before, and it didn't do much. It may have been because his kidneys were acting up at that time, so maybe this will be better. There isn't much else they can do for his belly, so we are hoping this will work.

The pain management folks were just there to evaluate him so that they can determine what pain medicine will work best for him at home. I hate to be sarcastic, but don't medicines work the same at any location? I'm sorry for that, but I have to laugh at something. They did have to go up on his morphine, and Paige said he was finally sleeping. Still no word on any possible shunt surgery, so we are thinking that it will not be tomorrow. The neurosurgeon is scheduled to come by today, so she is going to ask him when they are going to do it. I failed to mention earlier that his potassium is very low. They have him on an IV drip for that.

Well, that's all I have for now. If something changes, I'll let everyone know.

Matt

My weak attempt at humor in this update is nothing more than a curtain behind which to hide. As we learned new terms like "Palliative care" and "pain management" (which are the same thing, one just sounds better than the other), we were getting more familiar with other words such as sadness and grief. During this time, our friends began to surround us with love, nurses went the extra mile, and everyone seemed to want to walk with us down the dark road we were about to travel in earnest.

Nov 4, 2008

Everyone,

I just talked to Paige, and we still have no idea of when they are going to put his shunt in. They said maybe Thursday or Friday. I'll let everyone know for sure when we find out. The GI doctor said that he is going to try some more stuff that the other doctors have already tried to get his belly to go down. His belly is the same measurement today, but he did gain weight. He has a rash now all over his body. The doctors thought at first that it was a reaction to some of the medicine, but now think that it is part of his liver problems. His creatinine level is now back to normal, so that means that his kidneys are ok for now. I say ok for now, because, with his liver condition, it will eventually affect the blood flow to his kidneys.

The pain management people came by again today and told her that we would be going home with hospice to help manage his pain. He is still very uncomfortable right now, but hopefully, they can find the right amount of morphine to help him out. Maddie and I will be going up this evening and again for his birthday Thursday evening. Of course, all of this is dependent on how long Paige's mom holds on. She is the same as she has been the past few days.

That's all I have for now. If anything changes, or if some more doctors come by, I will update when I get up there later. Thank you for praying,

Matt

Maddie and I made the journey to the hospital after I had voted that morning at the Community Center. After spending the afternoon and most of the evening at the hospital with Paige and Elijah, we left around six to head home. Once in my truck, Maddie looked at me and asked if we could go see Maw Maw. I was tired and wanted to tell her no, but something in me took over. I smiled at her and said, "Of course, we can."

I turned the truck around, and I silently prayed for God to prepare Maddie's heart.

As we pulled into Randy and Donna's driveway, I

tried my best to prepare Maddie for what she would see. We walked up and into the house, and as we entered Donna's room, Maddie ran over and climbed up into her bed. She asked a few questions, and then she laid her head against Donna's and started telling her about her birthday party in the hospital room. As I watched Maddie, I prayed once again for God's hand of mercy for Donna. It had been five days since Donna took a turn for the worst, and I wondered how long her body would fight to survive. Her heart was the only thing keeping her alive; it seemed that it didn't want to stop. But then again, if you knew Donna, you knew that her heart was the biggest and strongest part of her. She was the most giving and loving woman I had ever met outside of my own mother.

Maddie and I pulled out of their driveway that evening around 10. We were exhausted from the day we had, and the long drive home seemed even longer than it usually did. The knowledge that Donna's time was near didn't help, but during those days, with a dying mother-in-law and a dying son, it was enough just to survive. One breath after another—we would make it through this somehow.

Nov 5, 2008

Everyone,

I just heard from Paige, and the neurosurgeon said that he is the second surgery tomorrow. It should be around 9 in the morning. The GI doctor says that he still wants to do some more medicine, so it will likely be next week before they get home. I'll believe it when I see them coming down the driveway. Also, they took some more blood yesterday, because they think his kidneys are acting up again. His urine output has not been good, and his legs and feet are starting to swell again. I know this is to be expected, but it doesn't make it any easier when it happens. I still have not given up on him. I did that twice before, so it will not happen again. (That is a long story) With that said, we also know that we cannot make him suffer for our benefit. For that reason, we have told the doctors that we do not want him resuscitated when he quits breathing. Most likely, he will be at home when that time comes, so it won't be an issue.

We have been asked to pick out the hospice we want for him, so Paige has been calling his pediatrician and his therapists. Hopefully, between them, they can tell us a good one for children. We obviously want only the best for him. There shouldn't be any more visits today, so this should be the only update today.

Also, Paige's mother is still hanging in there. Maddie and I stopped by there last night on our way home because she wanted to see her Maw Maw. Even though it was late, and I really wanted to get back home, I couldn't say no. She has not been conscious since Friday, so she has not had anything since then. I guess it's still minute to minute.

I want to thank everyone again for your prayers. I know I say that almost every time, but please know that it is a heartfelt "Thank you." We have been extremely blessed with the cards, emails, and phone calls. They are never a bother, and it touches my heart to know that Elijah's name is on so many hearts. I am very blessed,

Matt

It was also around this time that I received an unexpected phone call. Dennis Spaeth, a fellow member of our church, called me and started a much-needed conversation that I had not yet thought about. I was actually headed to the hospital to see Paige and Elijah when my phone started ringing.

"Hello?"

"Matt, this is Dennis Spaeth. Do you have time to talk?"

"Yes, sir."

"I know this is a difficult time, but I need to talk with you about a few things. Are you ok with that?"

"Absolutely, Mr. Dennis. We're good. What can I help you with?"

"I understand that Elijah's condition is terminal, is that right?"

"Yes, sir, it is."

"I'm sorry, Matt, and I hate to have to ask you this over the phone but have you and Paige thought about what Hospice organization you are going to use yet?"

"No, Sir. We have been looking but haven't been able to narrow it down. It is a bit overwhelming, to be honest."

"I'm not trying to steer you one way or another, but I am on the board of Baptist Hospice, and they are a great non-profit organization. I know you and Paige are dealing with insurance issues, so I wanted to let you know that you will never receive a bill from Baptist Hospice. You don't have to make any decision today. I just wanted to let you know that. You and Paige can make that decision when the time comes."

"Thank you, Mr. Dennis. I didn't know that at all. I will let Paige know, and when the time comes, can I just call you?"

"Of course, but there's something else I need to talk to you about as well."

"Ok."

"I know this is tough, and I don't know how else to say it. But when the time does come—when Elijah passes—please bring me any expenses you have in regards to his funeral."

"Mr. Dennis."

"Yes?"

"You don't have to do this. We're...."

"No, Matt. God has led me to. You don't have to worry about it. No one will ever know. As a matter of fact, please don't tell anyone."

"Mr. Dennis, I can't. This isn't something I can do."

"Matt, this isn't about you, me, or your son. This is about being obedient to God."

What do you say to that? How can you refute those words? How can you rob a blessing from someone who is simply trying to be obedient? That night, once I got home, I was adamant with God in my prayers. There wasn't any way I would let someone else pay for *my* son's funeral...are you kidding me? That simply isn't going to happen. But the more I prayed and thought about it, the more I realized that my selfish pride was getting in the way, and I was being a stumbling block to a wonderful man who was simply trying to follow God's leading. I ended our conversation by telling him that I would let him know later. We hadn't crossed that bridge yet, and I silently hoped God would answer my prayers in another, unexpected, way.

This brings me to another subject: answered prayer. God rarely answers our prayers in ways that we like or that make sense to us. Take this situation, for example. My prayers lined up with my needs. Insurance money was scarce, and our expenses were vast. During this time, bills seem to come from nowhere. For example, Paige's cell phone bill was normally $40. She has never used her phone much, so at that time, she had a plan that allowed for maybe 120 minutes or so a month. We didn't think to change it, and with it being her only way of communication in the hospital, she easily exceeded her monthly allowance. This resulted in a $400 cell phone bill that month that neither of us was prepared for.

Also, there was food, gas, and every other unexpected expense that you don't think of when someone is in the hospital. Children's Hospital only provided for Elijah, not Paige, so it fell to us to make up the difference.

I don't know about you, but when an $800 or more difference in what is going out every month hits, it makes things tight. If you combine that with all of Elijah's other medical bills and expenses, you don't have to go very far before any money you thought you had is gone.

So, it was with us during this time, and like any good Christian does, we prayed for God to help. How does He help in these situations? Does He rain money down from Heaven? Maybe you'll find a suitcase full of money on the sidewalk with a note that says, "Here you go. Thanks for praying...signed, God." You and I both know that's not how it works.

God works through his people, through people like Dennis Spaeth and all the others who felt led to shove money in an envelope and write our names on it. I learned one simple truth during this time. If you want

God to answer your prayers, you had better prepare your pride to take a hit. God will answer...always. But it may not be in the way you think. As a matter of fact, I would almost guarantee that it will never be as you think it will.

With that said, we'll move on to the next phase of these updates. Yes, God answers prayers, and sometimes that answer is, "No."

Maddie smiling for Daddy.

Elijah having fun

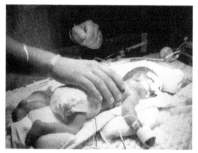

The first touch, when love broke through.

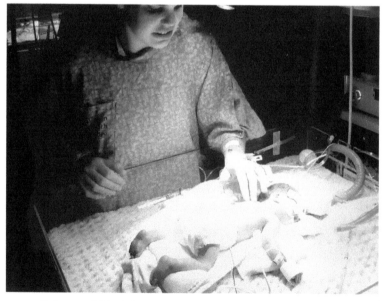

Paige and Maddie on her first day. November 2, 2004

Maddie and me. Bath time has always been a good time.

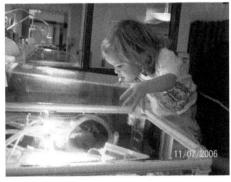

Maddie giving her "Bubba" a hug.

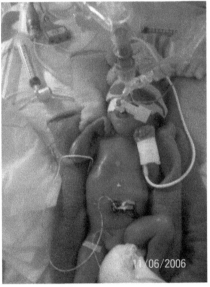

Elijah's first day November 6, 2006

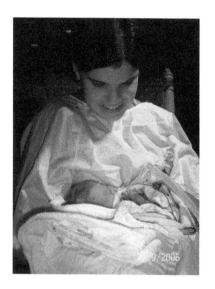

Elijah in his Christmas stocking.
Yes, it still hangs on our mantel
each year.

Celebrating Elijah's first Christmas morning in the NICU with Aunt
Brandi.

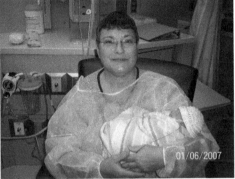

Paige's mother, Donna

My Dad holding the next Partain
man.

Maddie wanting "Bubba" to be quiet.

My mother singing to Elijah his song, Jesus Loves Me

Paige's Dad, Randy and Elijah

Finally going home! March 7, 2007

Elijah's headstone and footstone

Maddie giving Elijah a kiss. He thinks she is a bottle.

06/06/2008

June 6, 2008. I'm finally beginning to let God unlock the chains that were imprisoning my heart.

02/14/2008

One of the pictures from the NILMDTS photo session November 21, 2008

09/01/2008

Labor Day 2008 at the Wild Animal Safari in Pine Mountain, Georgia. This was the last "good" weekend.

Labor Day 2008 at the Wild Animal Safari
in Pine Mountain, Georgia. This was the
last "good" weekend.

Birthday celebration
2007. Maddie's third
and Elijah's first.

One of the pictures from the NILMDTS
photo session November 21, 2008

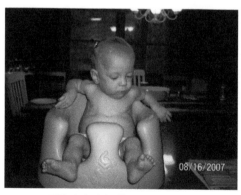

Elijah in his Bumbo chair

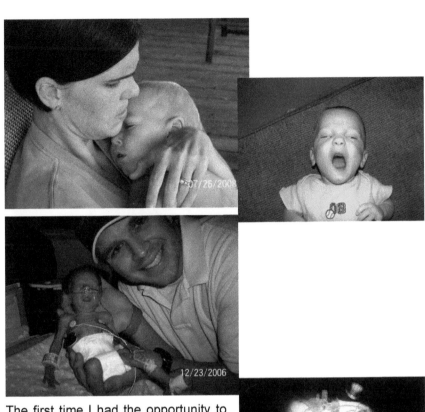

The first time I had the opportunity to pick him up.

The sign the nurses made for Elijah. November 6, 2008.

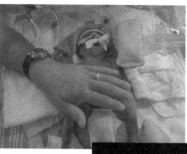

Trying to get him to eat apple sauce, but
all he wanted to do was get it everywhere.
Some of it went into his mouth.

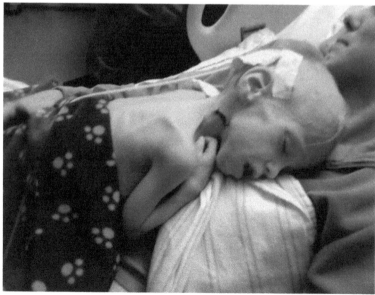

Elijah in the hospital. November 1, 2008

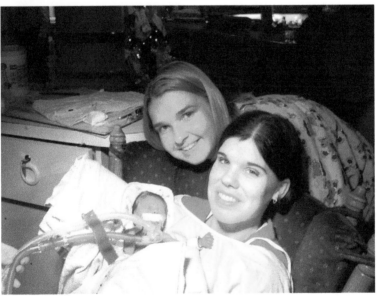

Paige's first-time holding Elijah.

Maddie serenading Elijah at the beach. I'm not sure what he enjoyed more, the singing or the sand.

The picture I shared in the April 27, 2017 Facebook post. Is God still good in the second picture?

Birthday celebration 2007. Maddie's third and Elijah's first.

Christmas Day 1976. I doubt anyone in this picture could have known how much it would come to mean to me. The six "Partain men" together. Grandpaw would pass four months later.

THE BEGINNING OF THE END

Lamentations 3:22-24 (NIV)
"Because of the Lord's great love we are not
consumed, for his compassions never fail. They
are new every morning; great is your faithfulness.
I say to myself, "The Lord is my portion; therefore
I will wait for him."

Nov 6, 2008

Everyone,

Happy Birthday, Elijah!!!

Elijah was taken back this morning at 7:30, and he came out of surgery at 9:00. He made it back into the room somewhere around 10:30. They had to put some more stitches in his head once he got into the room because the others had come out. Paige says that they are going home Monday no matter what. I think she has had enough of this place.

The GI doctors have come by, but there was so much going on that they are going to come back. I will update again whenever they round. We still haven't heard from the renal blood work they took the other day. His legs and feet are still swollen, so there is obviously something going on. His belly has been at 57 cm for the past four days, but he is continuing to gain weight. They are going to give him medicine this weekend for his belly, so we will see how that turns out.

That's all I have for now. I want to thank everyone again for their concern and prayers.

Matt

That morning, after Elijah's surgery, it was chaos in his room. The stitches in his head had pulled loose, and the doctor came in to sew them back in without giving Elijah anything for pain. I'm not sure I have ever seen Paige as upset as she was. The two of us held him, as he was screaming, so that the doctor could do his work. Neither of us was happy about the events that morning, and Paige was emphatic about taking Elijah home on Monday. She wasn't asking anymore. She was at her breaking point. She was done, plain and simple.

Nov 6, 2008

Everyone,

Ok, we've had all the doctors come by today, so here is the latest. The neurosurgeon says that his shunt looks good, and they are going to do a chest x-ray tomorrow to make sure it is in the right place. As far as they are concerned, he could go home tomorrow, but GI is keeping him until Monday. The pain management people came by again, and they are deciding what he needs to go home with. The GI doctor just left, and we finally got some concrete answers from him. He is going to do the albumin and Lasix again starting this evening. These are the medicines that have not worked in the past, but he is trying them again for three days just in case. We asked him about all the lab work, and nothing has come back yet. He told us that Elijah could not be a candidate for a liver transplant. His other organs (kidneys) give him problems anytime they try to treat his liver. Basically, if they started doing transplants, there would be no end to the problems that would show up in his other organs.

So, there is no doubt now that we are facing a terminal situation. I know this sounds terrible to everyone, but it's ok. He is God's child. We do not know how long we have with him. God has blessed us with two years so far, and just to have had the pleasure of being his daddy for one day would have been worth everything. I know that when he passes, our separation will only be temporary. We will see him again, and for the first time, he will see us clearly.

The nurses gave us a surprise today. When we came back up to the room, there was a Happy Birthday sign on Elijah's door and presents in the room. We were very surprised, and after a little while, they all came in with a cake and sang happy birthday to him.

This brings me to another subject. For most of these updates, I just say thank you for praying, but I don't think that could ever be enough. All of you have touched my family in a way that you could never imagine. The outpouring of love from everyone has overwhelmed us. Thank you for everything that you have done and continue to do. You are a blessing,

Matt

As I wrote those words, I was ignorant of the

emotional repercussions that come when you lose a child. I tried my best to be positive, but the faith I claimed had not been tested to the degree it was about to.

I can't say enough good things about the nurses who took care of us. As Elijah was in surgery and recovery, they were busy decorating his room. They hung balloons and made a poster board Happy Birthday sign. All of them had written messages to Elijah on it and had signed their names in love all over it.

As we entered the room, they sang Happy Birthday to him as Paige, and I wept. We were stunned by the love and compassion of those walking with us down the road no one wants to travel. We still have that sign, and anytime I look upon it and re-read those love notes, I get emotional again, and I'm taken back in time to that very special moment.

As I left the hospital that evening, my parents followed me home and stayed the night at my house. Maddie played with her Nannie as Dad, and I talked on the front porch in the swing. As I was digesting the day's events in casual conversation, my dad shifted his weight in the swing, turned towards me, and began to speak in a voice stricken with love.

"Son, I need to ask a favor of you."

"Yes, Sir."

"I don't know how else to say this...."

"Dad, what is it?"

"When the time comes. When...you know... can you please call *me*? Don't call your mother. I don't know how she will handle it. She has enough on her plate right now. Please, just call me, and let me be the one to tell her. I'm afraid she won't handle it well, and I need to be with her when she finds out. I need to be the one to tell her."

"Of course, Pop. I understand."

I will never forget that porch swing conversation with my father. It was one of the few times I was allowed to catch a glimpse of the deep love he has for my mother. Of course, I have always known that he loves her, but this simple conversation stunned me somewhat. The tenderness with which he spoke those words and how carefully he chose them made his request seem more like a friend to a friend instead of a father to a son.

Nov 7, 2008

Everyone,

I wanted to let everyone know that at 6:20 this morning, Donna went to be with Jesus. I am going to the hospital right now, and one of the nurses is staying with Elijah while Paige goes to be with her family. We are going to see if they will let Elijah go ahead and come home today or tomorrow. I will let everyone know as soon as I know something.

I was running in our field that morning, in the middle of my usual fifteen-lap workout, when I saw my father walking towards me. His head was bent down somewhat, and as I came near him, our eyes met, and I knew what had happened. I stopped, and before I could catch my breath, he said, "Donna is gone. She's gone home."

I thanked him for telling me, and I ran into the house to call Paige. She was already at her father's house, by her mother's bed, having left Elijah with one of Brandi's co-workers at the hospital who was getting off work. I tried my best to console her, but during these times, what can you really say? After ending our call, I hurried through a shower, got into my truck, and sped towards the hospital to care for Elijah.

Nov 7, 2008

Everyone,

As most of you know, Paige's mother passed away this morning at 6:20. They are going to make arrangements tomorrow at 12:00, so as soon as we know something, I will let everyone know. They are hoping to have the visitation Monday night and the funeral Tuesday afternoon. This might change after they meet with funeral home people tomorrow.

Elijah has had a rough morning. He has had a hard time breathing but has finally started to settle down. It may have been that I had him up while they were changing the sheets, but we're not sure. His belly grew 4 cm since yesterday, and he gained a lot of weight. The GI doctor came in and said that they are going to keep doing the medicines for his belly through today. If by tomorrow he has not lost a lot of the fluid, they are going to go ahead and let him leave because there is nothing else they can do. If they work, then they'll keep him for another round of the medicine on Sunday. The medicines have not worked before, so this is the last chance to get his belly down.

The pain management people have also come by and have started the process of getting everything ready for him to be discharged. He will not be home until Tuesday evening since Paige will be up here for the funeral. The neurosurgeon has not been by today, and they have not done the chest x-ray yet. There are no visible problems with his shunt like there were the last couple of times, so maybe this one will be ok.

That's all I have for now. Please continue to be in prayer for Paige and her family.

Matt

During the course of this day, God was setting things into motion that still awe me some eleven years later. As Paige and her family were making funeral arrangements, our church family was making plans on how to support us during this terrible time. They worked behind the scenes, and over the next few days, we would be surrounded by their love and compassion. God would use them to wrap His loving arms around us.

As I walked into Elijah's room, I thanked the nurse-friend of Brandi's, and I took Elijah into my arms. She explained that he had been extremely fussy and agitated since she had been in there, but it may have been because she wasn't Paige, and he knew it. After she left, his attitude didn't improve, and I gained a new respect for Paige and what she had been enduring the past 5 weeks in the hospital with him.

Of course, part of me thinks that he could sense something was off. He and Paige had a bond that couldn't be explained. I think he knew Paige was upset when she left, and that upset him. Whatever it was, he was not happy or calm until she returned later that evening.

Nov 8, 2008

Everyone,

They have made the arrangements for Donna. The viewing will be Monday night at Kilgore funeral home in Leeds from 6-8 PM. The following day at Bold Springs Presbyterian Church, there will a short viewing at 1 PM followed by the funeral at 2 PM.

Elijah has been sleeping most of the day. His belly went down, and he lost weight. That is wonderful news. They are going to do another day of those medicines and send him home with some to help with his belly. Anything that makes him more comfortable is a good thing. His shunt is still good, so there appears to be no problems with this one. He should get to leave Monday morning, but we will not get him home until Tuesday night after the funeral. I'm sure Paige will love to finally get home. She hasn't seen the place in a month.

Thank you all for your prayers.

Matt

After telling Dennis Spaeth that we were good using Baptist Hospice a few days earlier, he acted. Elijah was going to be discharged on Monday, but we would not be coming home until Tuesday evening at best. So, Dennis had two very nice ladies from Baptist Hospice come to the hospital in Birmingham that Sunday to make sure we had everything we needed and to see if we needed them to have someone come stay with us in Birmingham. After getting his hospice care lined up for Wednesday morning of that week, the ladies left, and Paige and I found some much-needed time to catch up with each other. Mom and Dad were bringing Maddie up later. I would stay at Paige's grandmother's house that evening before coming to get her and Elijah the next morning. It almost seemed too good to be true, but it looked as if we would finally be leaving the hospital together as a family.

Nov 11, 2008

Everyone,

I'm sorry I haven't gotten an update out to everyone lately, but Paige's parents don't have good internet access. The viewing last night and funeral today went well. In a way, it is a relief that Donna is no longer in pain and is with our Lord Jesus Christ. We do miss her, but we also know that she wouldn't come back if given the opportunity. I want to thank everyone for your prayers and for your support during this time. Your love has made this a lot easier to bear.

As far as Elijah goes, I will try and catch everyone up. I think the last update was Saturday, so here goes everything since then. His belly went down to 53 cm but has stayed there despite the medicine they are giving him. They have prescribed him some more to come home on so that maybe we can keep it smaller than it once was. He is off of the oxygen as of Saturday night, although Hospice has sent us home with a tank and a concentrator just in case we need them. He is still not eating well because his stomach is so crowded and because of the morphine. They have been giving him the morphine by mouth since Friday, and he has just started to act up. We are going to tell Hospice tomorrow that we need him back on the IV morphine to see if it helps him. He only eats one bottle in the course of a day when he used to eat six. Whenever he eats now, it's usually only 2 oz at a time, and since this morning, he has been bringing that back up after a few minutes.

On a couple of positive notes, he is smiling a little bit, and he is finally home! I wish that everyone could have seen him yesterday when we left the hospital. We started walking down the crosswalk, and he started looking around at everything. It was like he knew that he was getting out of that place. Then, the sun hit his face, and he began to smile. I know that had to feel good to him. It feels like it's been forever since I had all my chickens in the coop with me, but tonight feels almost normal again. Sometimes all we need to appreciate our family is some time without them.

Well, that's all I have tonight. Hospice will be by tomorrow to get to know us, so I'll send out an update after that. Thank you all for your prayers.

Matt

I wish I would have had a video camera. After the doctors had rounded that Monday morning, we finally had our walking papers, and you couldn't have knocked the smiles off our faces with a sledgehammer. We walked down the hallways of the hospital and rode the elevator down to the second floor. As we walked towards the parking deck, we came to a wall of windows that surrounded the glass crosswalk to the parking deck. As soon as we started across the crosswalk, the sun hit Elijah's face. Through the pain and confusion of all, he must have felt over the past month or so, he smiled. Paige and I stopped and looked at him. His face beamed as bright as the sun that shone on it, no doubt happy that he was leaving to go home. It's a picture my mind will never let go of.

Another part of those few days that I can't forget is how our church family loved us. I mentioned earlier that as Paige and her family were making arrangements for Donna's services, our church family was planning on how they could help us. One of those ways came in the form of one of our church friends, Jennifer Johnson. She came to the funeral home during Donna's visitation and again the next day as we held her funeral. She didn't say much other than she had come to take care of Elijah so that Paige could be where she needed to be. I will never forget the quiet, unassuming way she loved my family. Sometimes it's the little things that mean so much. I think Jennifer understood that. I know God used her to teach me a lesson I have not forgotten.

After Donna's funeral was over, the four of us made our way back home. For Paige, it was the first time she had been home in five weeks or so. We walked through the door to the familiar woodsy smell of our log home and were taken aback by more evidence of our church family's support. Our home was spotless.

Paige has always kept our home clean; even with two small children, there was never any clutter, and everything was always in its place. In her absence, I had kept it up as best I could, and to be honest, I was proud of the job I had done. I'm sure it wasn't up to her standards, but hey, I did the best I could.

But we both knew something had been done when we walked in. It wasn't until later that I learned that some of the ladies of our church had come by and cleaned our home from top to bottom. Again, it's the little things sometimes that bless the most.

Nov 12, 2008

Everyone,

Elijah did not rest well last night. He and Paige were up most of the night, but he has been a little better today. It's just hard for him to get comfortable at this point. He hasn't brought any of his food back up today, but he has only taken in 4 oz of formula.

The admissions nurse from hospice came by today, and he was extremely nice. He didn't act like he was in a hurry, and he took a lot of time getting to know Elijah. The regular nurse will be by tomorrow. They are going to change him to a morphine dissolvable that goes under his tongue. I guess it's like one of those Listerine things that make you think your mouth is in hell. Yes, you know, the ones that would make an opossum's breath smell fresh. Anyway, they're using something like that.

I asked the nurse about Elijah's condition, and he has seen it before. He gave us a pretty good picture of what we've got ahead of us. I have read a lot about it on the Internet, and everything points to us having a few weeks to a couple of months left with him. We'll make the best of it and cherish every second.

Well, that's all I have for today. After the nurse comes by tomorrow, I will update again. I also want to thank those people who have helped us out. You know who you are. I have had to learn a hard lesson about my pride, and I thank God for it. You are a blessing, and I thank God for people who listen as He gently whispers.

Matt

Drew was the admissions nurse that came by that day. He described for us, in detail, what our son's illness would do to him, and I was extremely grateful for his honesty. We had seen enough already to know that nothing about this would be easy, but it helped to have an honest road map of where we were headed.

Elijah slept on Paige's chest in our bed that night, no doubt a holdover from them being in the hospital together for so long. It was difficult for either of them to get much rest, but I'm sure it was a relief for both to be home.

The last part of that update mentions those who have helped us out. At this point, our bills were well beyond our ability to pay them. We were struggling to make all our frayed ends meet, but once again, our church family stepped willingly into the pit we found ourselves in. For every unexpected bill, there was a prayer, and for every prayer, there was an answer in the form of someone helping us out. My pride didn't want to receive it, but how could I refuse an answered prayer and rob a blessing from someone who was obedient to what God had prompted them to do?

Nov 13, 2008

Everyone,

Today has been a better day for Eli. He slept well last night, which means Paige did also. He has been fussy at times, but that's to be expected. He mostly just lays on top of one of us and takes it easy. That's perfectly alright with both Paige and me, and I think we can afford to spoil him just a little bit. He has only eaten 5 ounces today, so that's not good. There again, it's to be expected.

The Hospice nurse came by today twice, and she is very nice. She removed his pic line because it was not working. We really don't need it at this point. It was there just in case they needed to stick him for any reason, but it is very doubtful that they will need to now. Everything is centered around making him comfortable, so needles are out as long as everything can be taken care of by mouth.

There's really nothing new to tell, and I imagine it will be this way for a while. I feel like we are in the calm before the storm, and one day everything will start to happen all at once. I will still keep this updated, and I hope you keep praying.

Also, I wrote another blog on my myspace page. It kind of tells you all the things I have wanted to write here but don't have the space for. Anyway, it's nothing special, but if you want to, you can read it.

Still praising Him,

Matt

Our Hospice nurse, Lori, was a Godsend. I have often said that even though Elijah couldn't have been her only patient, it sure felt like he was. I asked her the same questions I had asked Drew the day before. I wanted to know what we were in for and what I needed to look out for as his illness progressed. She told us that by looking at him, she thought we had anywhere from a month to six weeks. I swallowed hard at the thought of such a short time frame. She then talked about what she called a "blessing time." Most folks think of it as "getting better before they die," but that's not how she put it to us.

She told us of other children she had cared for and how almost all of them had suddenly gotten better just before passing away. We would likely see Elijah as he used to be; he may laugh as he used to and behave more like we remembered before becoming sick. I cataloged all she said in my mind because I wanted to be ready for whatever came next. I simply had no idea that no amount of foreknowledge could prepare me for the days that lay ahead.

Nov 14, 2008

Everyone,

Today Elijah has had a pretty good day. We took him out to the Mexican restaurant and then to the craft show at the civic center. He was doing ok until I let him eat too much at the craft show. You can imagine what happened after that.

He still can only take about 2 or 3 ounces at a time, and he doesn't eat very often. His belly isn't that swollen, so it might be the morphine that is making him sick. The Hospice people brought some medicine by today to help with that, so we'll see how it works. I know he will get a lot thinner, but it hurts to think that he will look even worse than he does now.

We are going to bring him to church Sunday, but only for the second worship service. For all of you who will be there, please know that he does not look like he used to.

Well, that's all I have for today. Thank you for your words of encouragement and everything else that you are doing. Everyone one of you are an inspiration to me, and I appreciate you far more than words could ever say.

Also, Ben Emfinger, you are a crazy man, but I love you and your heart. You will never know how much you blessed me Wednesday night.

See you tomorrow,

Matt

The craft show I mentioned is the annual Charis Crafters Christmas sale. Paige was a member at that time, but for obvious reasons couldn't take part in it. We went, not only to support the ladies there but to allow them to see the child they had been praying for. In a way, I guess we wanted them to be able to say their goodbyes to him before it was too late.

Ben Emfinger is a young man in our church, and at the time, was in our youth group. He had beautiful, long, curly, flowing hair but had told people he would cut it off if he could raise enough money for Elijah. I don't remember the amount, but I remember the sacrifice Ben made because he loved us. It seemed that our church family helped us through every hard part of this journey. They were in step with us, locking arms and supporting us as we grew ever closer to the day we all dreaded.

Nov 15, 2008

Everyone,

Elijah had a bad morning but seems to be doing better this evening. Paige's dad, grandmother, and my parents are here, so there has been no shortage of attention for him or Maddie. His belly measurement was 40 cm. That's extremely good considering that it was 53 cm just a few days ago. While that is good news, he still has only eaten 2 ounces of food today, and he tried to bring that back up. It seems the medicine that we are giving him for nausea has had no effect on it, but we're going to give it some more time. It may work yet, although I don't know if it will help his appetite.

As far as his pain goes, something is still hurting him pretty bad. We couldn't get him comfortable this morning until we gave him more morphine ahead of the schedule he is on. It doesn't matter about the schedule to me if he's hurting.

Well, that's all I have for today. Paige will have him at church tomorrow for the second service if he does ok through the night. I didn't know if we should bring him or not, but we are not going to keep him from you or keep you from him. There have been too many prayers lifted up by you, and sometimes it's good to see what you're praying for. Please remember, however, that he does not look the same. He has lost a lot of weight. Anyway. We'll see you tomorrow.

Matt

If you've ever been through a hospice situation, you can relate somewhat to what I've written. Your goal is to keep your loved ones comfortable as they die, so you walk a thin line between too little and too much pain medication. No matter what you do, you feel like you're not doing the right thing. The more pain medicine you give, the more they sleep. Too little, and they're in pain. You selfishly want them to be awake, but all too often, being awake means being in pain. What do you do? The answer is, you do the best you can. You survive, and you take each minute as it comes.

Nov 16, 2008
Everyone,
I'm sorry that Elijah and Paige didn't make it to church today. It's been a really bad 24 hours. He has done

nothing but scream since last night, and no amount of pain medicine has helped. We think that maybe it was his stomach because after a couple of bad (and I mean BAD) diapers, he has finally started to rest a little. He is still only eating a couple of ounces at a time, so he is losing a lot of weight. Hopefully, we can get him to church this next Sunday.

They will be headed back to Birmingham tomorrow. Paige, Maddie, and Elijah are spending the night with her grandmother and then going to Children's to get his stitches out on Tuesday. This is also the follow-up appointment for the shunt surgery. I will update tomorrow to let everyone know how he is doing. Thank you all for your prayers.

Matt

I was extremely disappointed that we couldn't take him to church. I knew in the back of my mind that we had likely missed the only opportunity we would have to take him there before he passed. Elijah was losing weight at an alarming rate, and by this time, his features became more skeletal. He looked nothing like he did just a month and a half earlier, and it pained me to see him go downhill so quickly.

Nov 17, 2008
Everyone,
Elijah did fair today. The hospice nurse came by and gave us some medicine since he was very agitated. This seemed to calm him down a lot or at least made him less likely to scream at the slightest noise or movement. We have also switched back to his original formula just to see if the new stuff was the reason he was getting sick. I know

that liver failure causes lack of appetite and nausea, but it's not going to hurt anything to try this for his comfort. He has only taken in four ounces today, but maybe tomorrow will be better. Part of me is still waiting for him to turn the corner and get better, but the other part prays for mercy. It's a difficult situation, but one that we just came out of with Paige's mother. It's a strange and winding road, but it makes perfect sense to God. He's the driver, and I trust Him.

They are on their way to Birmingham for his appointment tomorrow with the neurosurgeon. Maddie was looking forward to a day with Paige's grandmother. She gets to tear her house up with no consequences.

Anyway, that's all I have for tonight. I'll update again tomorrow evening. Thank you again for all your thoughts and prayers.

Matt

I had no way of knowing it then, but the "blessing time" Lori had told us about was beginning.

Nov 18, 2008
Everyone,
Elijah has had a great day! He has eaten 14 ounces and has rested peacefully. Paige said he was a little fussy this morning, but after getting a bottle, he started to settle down. They got back from Birmingham around 5 this evening, and after taking 5 ounces, he went right to sleep. I guess he's making up for the sleep he lost this past weekend. We're thinking that the other formula they wanted him on was making his stomach hurt, so we've put him back on what he was on before he went into the hospital. Even

though he is still not getting enough to sustain him, we are happy that he is happy. We'll take a good day and praise God for it. It seems like an eternity since we had a good one, so we're going to enjoy every moment of this one.

I almost forgot about the doctor's visit. Everything is fine with his shunt, and they took the last of his stitches out. He still looks a little like Frankenstein, but he's a cute one.

Well, that's all I have for now. Hopefully, Elijah will rest tonight. I know he needs it.

Matt

I can't begin to explain what a good day meant for us as a family. He wasn't constantly screaming, and he seemed content most of the day. You really can't appreciate those small blessings unless you've walked a while in those shoes.

Nov 19, 2008

Everyone,

Elijah has had another good day today. He actually drank 9 ounces at one time this morning but only has taken in another 5 since. That's the same amount (14oz) as yesterday, but we'll take it. Also, he has rested some more today and has been really good. He's fussed at times, but he gets that from his Momma anyway. I think that medicine we have been giving him for agitation has really helped. Anyway, that's all I have for today.

Like I said a few days ago, I think we're kind of in the calm before the storm. Everything seems to have slowed down a bit, and the main thing is that he is comfortable. This would be a lot worse if every day was like this past

Sunday. Thank you all for your prayers and for caring about my son. We'll talk to you tomorrow.

Matt

My 33rd birthday was spent mostly at home. I went into work but came home soon after, not wanting to miss any of the time I had left with Elijah. After church that night, I came home and told Paige that we needed to get out of the house as a family. For some reason, we decided to go out on the next day, a Thursday. I decided to call in sick to work for the next day, and as Elijah drifted off to sleep on Paige, we talked about where we would go and what we would do.

She also informed me that she had decided to have Elijah's picture professionally taken by an organization, *Now I Lay Me Down to Sleep*. These people come into your home and take beautiful photos of children that have a terminal diagnosis. Brandi had told Paige about it, so she had scheduled the session for Saturday. We wanted to have at least one good set of pictures before he was gone.

Nov 20, 2008

Everyone,

Elijah has had another good day today. He has eaten almost 20 ounces today and has only fussed a couple of times. We have only had to give him morphine twice today. He is still hurting some, but not as bad as he was.

Also, he is sleeping more, but that is another one of the symptoms of liver failure. He has been smiling some, and we almost got him to laugh this morning. Maddie has a special way with him and can get him to smile over almost anything. It is wonderful to see those two interact with one another. This is a good time for us, and we'll have no problem this Thanksgiving finding things to be thankful for. He is good, and I still praise His name. I always will.

Matt

That morning, after calling in to work, Paige and I got the kids dressed and prepared to go out. We drove to Prattville, which is about 30 minutes away, and ate a late breakfast at IHOP. Of course, a few people stared at him and us, and our waitress asked us about him. We briefly told her his story, and you could see how uncomfortable she became when we talked about his terminal condition. I don't remember her words after that, but I remember the saddened look she left our table with.

Afterward, we shopped in a few stores and then returned home after eating a late lunch. The highlight of our day was Maddie singing to Elijah in his car seat on the way to Prattville. He thought the voice she made was funny, and he almost managed a full-fledged laugh. We cherished the wide smile that ran across his face; it is one of the many wonderful memories of that very unusual day.

Once we were at home, Paige decided to pull out our Christmas tree and decorate a little for Christmas. Normally, we wouldn't break out the first Christmas decoration until after Thanksgiving, but for reasons still unknown to us, we decided to put up our tree, decorate it, and sing Christmas songs along with the CD in the radio.

For a few wonderful hours that evening, we were

a normal family again. Death and sadness were beaten back by the joy of simply being together. I held Elijah as Maddie and Paige decorated the tree. All seemed right in our world for the first time in a long while, and I relished the present God had given us under that tree. As we turned in for the night, I once again thanked God for the blessing He had given before drifting off into a peaceful sleep.

The next morning, I awoke at my usual time and went running in our field. I came in, showered, and got dressed for work. I kissed my family goodbye before walking out of the quiet house to start what I was sure would be a busy and hectic Friday. My ten-minute drive to work was filled with a prayer of thanks for the previous few days, and I walked into the room we gather in every morning with a grateful smile on my face and a little spring back into my step.

The guys at work wanted to know the latest on Elijah, so I filled them in on the past few day's events. As we talked, my phone rang, and I looked down and saw that it was Paige. I flipped it open to answer it, and as the speaker met my ear, I could tell something was once again horribly wrong.

"Hello?"

"Matt, you need to come home now! Elijah has thrown up blood...it's everywhere! I don't know how much longer he's going to hold on! Please hurry! Get here as fast as you can!"

"I'm on my way."

We knew something like this was coming, but that still made it no easier. I ran outside of the office to my truck and floored the accelerator. I didn't know if Elijah would still be alive, but I didn't feel like there was much time. I made a few frantic calls to our family on the way to the house, and the short ten-minute drive was likely only six or seven minutes.

I slid my truck to a stop in the gravel driveway and ran inside. I yelled for Paige, and she answered from the kitchen. Turning the corner in the hallway, I wasn't prepared for the scene that met my eyes.

Elijah was pale, a deathly white color, and was barely breathing. There was a massive amount of blood on the kitchen floor, and both he and Paige were covered in it as well. I didn't know what to do; neither of us did. She called Lori, our hospice nurse, as well as the other people who needed to know.

As our family began to head our way, the four of us sat down on the sofa in the living room, waiting on the inevitable. Paige and I held Elijah together with Maddie beside us. As we watched him gasp for air, we took the time to tell him exactly what was on our hearts and told him that it was OK for him to go. We sang to him, prayed over him, and spoke to him the words that all of us needed to hear. It was a special time for us. Once people started arriving at our home, I took the time to update the CaringBridge site.

Nov 21, 2008

Everyone,

Elijah has taken a turn for the worse this morning. He started vomiting large amounts of blood and breathing very shallow in between. He has since stabilized, and although he is pale and cold, he is hanging on. All of this is symptoms of liver failure. We have called in our family, and we are just waiting to see what's going to happen. Please be in prayer for us as we go through this time. I will update again later this evening or when something else happens.

Still praising Him,

Matt

During this terrible day, Paige called the photographer, Judy Barranco, with NILMDTS to tell her that Elijah might not make it until the scheduled time the next day. To her credit, the photographer dropped whatever she was doing and headed our way. Once she arrived, we were able to take the pictures that are still cherished to this day. Their ministry is a special one, and it has given my family memories that will last forever.

Other people came to our home that day to be by our side. Some of our church family, even those to who we weren't necessarily close, felt led to come to our home. One of those men was Bill Coleman. He came by, and although he didn't say much, his presence was enough. That simple act taught me a lot about ministering to people in times of grief. Sometimes all you need to do is be there.

Our family stayed until bedtime that evening. After promising to call them should anything change, they left until the next morning. Before turning in myself, I updated the site one more time.

Nov 21, 2008

Everyone,

Elijah is still about the same as the last update. He

is stable, but his breathing is irregular. He'll take a breath and then wait sometimes as long as 5 or 6 seconds before taking another. He is pretty much out of it and has not eaten anything today. He only makes a sound whenever you move him, and even then, he only protests for a few seconds before settling back down.

On a positive note, he is no longer cold like he was this morning, and he has not vomited again. We are just waiting on and praying for God's will. We had a special time this morning with him before anyone got here. Paige, Maddie, and I talked to him, prayed over him, and sang his favorite song to him. We all said what was on our hearts, and just to have that time with him is a blessing from God.

Please continue to pray for us and for our family. We are so thankful for each and every one of you, and even though I don't know some of you, you still are a blessing to my family. I will update again tonight if anything changes, but otherwise, it will be tomorrow morning. Thank you again for your prayers and for all that you have done.

Matt

Nov 22, 2008

Everyone,

Elijah had a bad night. He was very agitated and wouldn't lay still. His breathing was still irregular and has worsened this morning. He is laboring pretty hard just to take a breath, and the nurse has started him on some more medicine to try and help him. We have also started giving him more morphine because it was evident that he was starting to feel more pain. Another symptom appeared last night in the form of him passing blood in his diaper. He has not vomited again, but it appears that he is still losing blood. He did eat a little last night and again this morning, so that's the only positive news I have right now. If anything changes, I will update again. Thank you again for your prayers.

Matt

This was starting to get even more difficult to watch. On this day, our home was once again filled with our family and friends as we waited on the inevitable to come to pass. His Pediatrician, Dr. Fekete, came by to visit him as well, and it was further enforced that we were blessed to have her as a doctor to our children. For the most part, however, it was just our family, minus my brother, and the Stuarts, who stayed the day.

As usual, I kept in contact with my brother and told him that he was not needed just yet. With him still being on active duty in the Navy, I knew that he needed to save what leave time he had. Besides, his young girls didn't need to see their cousin in this condition.

That evening was the same as the day before, with our family staying until very late. We tried to sleep that night after everyone left, but I'm not sure we did. How could we?

Nov 23, 2008

Everyone,

Elijah made it through the night, so we'll see what happens today. Yesterday afternoon he could no longer swallow, so he has not had anything to eat since yesterday morning. His breathing is still very labored and sometimes is accompanied by a snoring sound. I think that is because he is having to breath so heavily. He has not been awake since yesterday morning, but I don't think he is completely out of it. He still knows when he is moved and when it's time for his medicine. We are having to give him morphine a good bit now, but I guess that's to be expected. Well, that's all I have for this morning. Thank you for your prayers,

Matt

I remember writing that update. I broke down in desperate prayer, crying to God to be merciful to my son. His suffering was more than I could take, and I desperately wanted God to act. It's a terrible thing to ask God to take your son, but given the sight before my eyes, there was no other choice. Elijah, my precious boy, was in terrible pain and agony, and there wasn't anything I could do to alleviate it. So, I prayed and wept uncontrollably. I couldn't help it. The tears and sobs could not be held back any longer.

Nov 23, 2008

Everyone,

Elijah has been about the same today. He cannot swallow, and he is unconscious for the most part. His shallow breathing is still very labored, and sometimes there are 10 seconds or more between his breaths. His is starting to get even more cool to the touch, and his lower body is very stiff. I guess all these things are signs that he will not be with us much longer.

I am still praying for mercy, but God knows what He's doing. His ways are not our ways, and I trust Him to be the perfect Father that He is. I would lie if I said that this wasn't getting a lot tougher, but our strength has never been our own. It comes from The Father, and He is still blessing us during this time.

I will always look upon the time we have had with Elijah as one of the most blessed in my life. And when this is over, I will look at this time in the same way. His blessings never stop, but I think sometimes we stop looking for them.

We'll see you tomorrow,

Matt

We went to bed knowing that Elijah would likely not make it through the night. Paige lay next to me with Elijah on her chest, just as she had done since they came home from the hospital. Maddie slept between us that night, but Paige and I were restless. If we found sleep at all, it wasn't for long. Each time one of us awoke, we would lay our hand on his back, and each time we did, we felt his chest rise and fall. He was still breathing, and as the sun began to filter through the windows, I went into the bathroom to get ready for the day.

I didn't run that Monday morning, and I wasn't planning on going in to work either. I knew people would start arriving before long, so I couldn't lay in the bed any longer. Still exhausted, both physically and mentally, I staggered to the bathroom. After taking a shower and getting ready, I walked over to Paige, who was still in the bed with Elijah on her chest and Maddie by her side.

I asked her if he was still breathing as I placed my hand on his back again. Before she could answer, I felt his chest rise and fall. As he exhaled, something felt different. It was longer and more pronounced. I waited for his chest to rebound and for his body to take in more air, but I didn't feel it rise again under my hand. I waited a few extra seconds before I said anything, but in my heart, I knew my son had just met Jesus.

"Baby, I think he's gone."

"No, no, he was just breathing."

"No, Baby. I think he's gone."

Paige rolled quickly off the bed as she placed him on top of the blanket on his back. His fight was over. Ours was just beginning. Paige woke Maddie, and through tears, told her that her brother was with Jesus. She crawled over to Paige's side of the bed, her eyes still half shut, and we placed Elijah in her arms. She looked at him, love flowing through her still sleepy eyes, and as my knees hit the floor, I lifted my broken voice in prayer.

Paige knelt beside me, one arm around me and the other on Elijah. Through sobs and tears, I thanked God for my son, for his life, and for giving us the blessing his life was. I hadn't planned that moment, but under the circumstances, there was nowhere else to turn, nowhere else to look but up.

After getting off my knees, I dialed my father's number. He answered, and I told him that Elijah was gone. I'm not sure what else was said in that brief conversation, but Dad was, as usual, a rock, just as he has always been. He always knows what to say and where to be. He's solid, and no matter the situation, I've always been able to count on him. My next call was to my brother. I knew he would have to get his girls out of school and start the long drive in our direction.

My mother was already at work. She worked in the Circuit Clerk's office at the courthouse. She was just starting her Monday morning when she looked up at the customer window and saw my dad standing there.

By the look he gave her, she knew instantly. From what I know of her reaction, I'm glad he was there.

After hanging up with my brother, I called Paige's father, sister, and the hospice nurse. After making the last of my calls, I went to the computer to type out the message no one wanted to read but that everyone knew was coming.

Nov 24, 2008

Everyone,

Elijah went to be with Jesus this morning around 7:30. Praise God for my son! Praise God for his life! He is not hurting anymore. As soon as we make arrangements, I will let everyone know what they are. Thank you all for your prayers.

Still praising Him,

Matt

Once everyone arrived at our home, members of the family took turns holding Elijah's earthly vessel. Around mid-morning, the local funeral home's hearse was outside, and Paige carried him in his favorite blanket to the car. She placed him inside, and we watched the long black car drive slowly down the driveway.

Shortly after, Paige's dad drove us to Kilgroe Funeral Home in Leeds, because they were closest to where he would be buried. Living an hour and a half from where we grew up made the logistics a little difficult, and with it being the week of Thanksgiving, we knew that might make it even more so. The 90-minute drive was spent mostly in silence. Not much more could be said.

We arrived at the funeral home. As we started

discussing options with them, my mind was taken back to Dennis Spaeth and his insistence that he pay for my son's funeral.

I was surprised to learn that the funeral home didn't charge for a lot of their services because it was a child. It seems that society realizes that it is a terrible thing to outlive your children. We left Kilgroe Funeral Home a little after lunch and headed back to our house to meet with our Pastor, Gary Miller, and our Worship Pastor, Randy Godfrey, so that we could plan the service.

> Nov 24, 2008
> Funeral Arrangements:
> Visitation will be at Santuck Baptist Church Tuesday, Nov. 25 from 5:00-8:00pm
> Funeral will be at Santuck on Wednesday at 11:00am. There will be childcare for this service.
> Graveside services will be in Leeds, Alabama at Bold Springs Presbyterian Church. There will be a short viewing in the church from 3-4 pm, with the graveside service in the cemetery at 4:00.
> Thank you for your continued love and prayer for this family.

The meeting at our dining table with Gary and Randy went about as well as I thought it could. I told Brother Gary that I wanted to speak before his sermon. I felt that those who would be there needed to hear from one of us. With Brother Randy, we picked out a couple of songs we thought would best fit the service. Of course, we wanted *his* song, "Jesus Loves Me," sang, but also a Casting Crowns song entitled, "And Now My

Lifesong Sings."

The Casting Crowns song is not the upbeat one you've heard on the radio. It's the subtle one, the last song, on the same album. It seemed to fit the service and the life of our son.

That night, after everyone had left, the house was quiet and still. Paige and I spoke of Elijah and of the plans for the next few days. Thanksgiving was going to be tough, and I hoped to be able to live out the faith I had claimed thus far. Maddie played around with her toys, and we kept our minds occupied with her as best we could. As we turned in for the night, my mind took me back to that hotel pool in Georgia and the miracle God had worked the next day in that filthy restroom. I wondered what this day would have looked like without that one, and as my exhausted body and mind finally shut down, I thanked God one more time for His grace and the life of my son.

The next evening, we arrived at the church early for our family viewing time, and I was met with another surprise. An old family friend, Terry Wilson, was there. Mr. Terry attended the church I grew up in and worked for the same company that owned Kilgroe Funeral Home. I learned that he had been the one that prepared Elijah's body and made sure everything was done as we requested.

Elijah's casket was placed on the Lord's Supper table in the Sanctuary. After we entered, we each took a few moments to gather our emotions as the reality of the situation took hold. Just before 5 pm, we made our way back beside his casket as the doors were opened to allow people to come pay their respects. It wasn't long before the line of people trickled out of the sanctuary and into the church's foyer. During this three-hour period, there was an endless stream of those that came to support us in one of our darkest hours. I remember only a few of those who spoke to us, and I'll save one of those stories for a little later.

That night, once again exhausted, I tried to prepare what I would say the next day, but my mind was still too numb to function. I finally found sleep that night, but not before losing control of myself once again. I would later learn that these waves of grief and sadness begin slowly but build over time. These unexpected moments were just the ripple of what was to come later down the road of life.

The next morning, we were getting ready for the long day ahead, and to my surprise, I was able to muster up enough words to put on paper for my part of the service. We gathered at the church around ten that morning and, as a family, waited in one of the Sunday School rooms just outside the Sanctuary. At eleven, we entered the sanctuary as our pianist, Susan Philips, played "Amazing Grace." When it came time for me to address everyone, I swallowed hard and walked up behind the cross-shaped pulpit.

I simply read what I had written down, and it was Elijah's story. I didn't know what else to say. As I read through what I had written, I felt something deep inside me move. The Holy Spirit whispered, and I listened. Once I had reached the end of what I had written down, I looked up, locked eyes with my wife, and I spoke my heart to her. I don't remember what was said. It wasn't planned. It was just my heart speaking to hers with a lot of people there to witness it.

After the service at Santuck, we ate lunch in the Fellowship Hall. In usual Baptist fashion, there was enough food to feed an army, but there was also a group of men who had a special treat for me.

I was fortunate to be a part of a group of men that ate lunch together every Wednesday. We met at Bush's Grocery, a small convenience store on the outskirts of the small town of Eclectic. Jonathan Stuart and I started meeting there several years before, but the group had grown to include most of our church ministerial staff as well. So it was that I found myself around a table after my son's funeral with those same men, enjoying a Bush's hamburger. Chad Middlebrooks, our Youth Pastor at the time, had bought each of us a hamburger and brought them to the church.

After our lunch, we rode to Leeds with Jonathan and Christy Stuart. I couldn't imagine making that long trip with anyone else. They had walked every single mile of Elijah's life with us, so it was only fitting that we take the final journey of it with them. They were more than friends at this point. They were family. One would think that the hour and a half drive would have been somber, but the ride was cheerful and joyful as we recounted the many blessings of God we had experienced over the past couple of years.

Once inside the small beautiful sanctuary of Bold Springs Presbyterian church, we readied ourselves for yet another time for receiving people. It was, again, an endless stream of people that came to pay their respects to us. While most of them had never met Elijah, they knew us from the brief time we lived in Leeds. Once that was over, it was time to carry my son's body to its final resting place just beside the church.

There were four of us pallbearers: my dad, Paige's dad, Jonathan Stuart, and myself. We each took a corner of the casket and made our way carefully down the path to the cemetery. It's a peaceful, quiet, and beautiful place, right beside Lake Purdy, underneath huge stately oaks. Once we made it to the graveside, we placed Elijah's coffin on the straps of the hoist and made our way to the chairs provided for us.

My parent's pastor spoke at the graveside. I couldn't tell you what he said, but I remember that he read a poem written by my brother's youngest daughter, Jocelyn. After a prayer, the service was concluded, and we went back inside to eat supper as the gravediggers did their work.

Thirty minutes later, I received word from Ron Parsons, a family friend, that they had finished covering the grave. It was over. All over. That's what I thought at that moment, but I was wrong. In my mind, I wanted to put a bow on this time of our lives and call it finished, over and done with, but I couldn't have been more mistaken. Sure, the living and breathing part of Elijah's life was over, but the most difficult part of mine was just beginning.

We rode back to Santuck with Jonathan and Christy again and went home to get ready to drive right back up near Birmingham the following day. It would be Thanksgiving, and we were still going to be as thankful as we could, despite the circumstances we were in. Before turning in, I updated the page one last time.

Nov 27, 2008

Everyone,

I just wanted to say thank you to everyone who has prayed for us these past couple of months. You have been an inspiration to me, and we have felt your prayers. They have helped us and lifted us up in our time of need. We are truly blessed and very thankful to our Lord for Elijah. He is a special little boy. Also, I have been asked to post a copy of what I said at Elijah's funeral, so if you want to see it, please go to www.myspace.com/mnppartain and look for the blog. Thank you all again, and I would like to ask that you continue to pray for us.

Matt

The following day, Thanksgiving, was spent in a numbing haze. Think of it as simply going through the motions of life. We were spent, both physically and emotionally, and had no strength left to feel anything.

We ate lunch at my Aunt Sharon's home and then dinner at Paige's grandmother's. The day was a somber one. Sure, there was laughter here and there; but for the most part, we simply survived the day as best we could.

The next day we slept in. Around mid-morning, my brother and his family came down to our house, and he and I changed out the brakes on Paige's car. It was nice to allow my mind to take a break as my hands went to work. I once again found common ground with my grandfather, enjoying the time I had with my brother.

His family stayed the night with us, and after all of our girls had turned in for the night, my brother and I sat in our living room and talked about Elijah. In the stillness of the evening, we talked and cried together, remembering and reliving the past few years.

I didn't know until that evening that my brother had dreams wrapped up in Elijah as well and that he was as excited as I was in having another Partain boy in the family. A little after midnight, we turned in, and I went to sleep thankful once again for my brother's counsel.

Over the next few weeks, the busyness of life between Thanksgiving and Christmas began to encompass our lives. We attended a remembrance service for Elijah in Leeds on the 4th, I was playing the drums in our church's Christmas musical on the 7th, and I was asked to speak at Baptist Hospice's Christmas concert on the 16th. But before that, we were given a surprise by my mom and dad's church. They had taken up a collection for us with the stipulation that we use it to go on a short trip out of town. I'm not sure how they knew that was needed; however, to this day, I am still thankful for their generosity.

We left for Gatlinburg, Tennessee, with a stop in Brasstown, North Carolina, on the 10th. Over the next couple of days, we enjoyed the time we spent together. It seemed that our attitudes towards life had changed somewhat. We understood, to a degree, the fragility of life; so, we soaked in the moments with each other, fully realizing that we're never guaranteed another.

On the Sunday before Christmas, the 21st, I spoke at my parent's church. I told Elijah's story once again, and I thanked them for the gift they had given us. I remember saying, "The trip was used for healing," not knowing the ignorance with which I spoke. Healing?

Really? If I could go back and talk to myself that day, I would kindly tell the younger me that you have no idea what you're talking about. A month had yet to pass since Elijah died, and I'm talking about healing already. How was I to know that we were still living under the supernatural grace that God provides parents like us? As time passed, I would understand that fact, and I would learn just how foolish the talk of healing this soon really was.

MOVING FORWARD-
LEARNING TO GRIEVE

1 Corinthians 15:55 (NIV)
"Where, O death, is your victory?
Where, O death, is your sting?"

As I write this part of the book, I want to let you know that this has been written over the course of several years. In fact, as I type this, I am a little more than eleven years further down the road of life. In some ways, it's hard to believe it's been that long, but in others, it feels like an eternity ago. When the waves of grief roll in every October through December, the pain is still just as fresh as it has always been. In contrast, when I think back to what made my son who he was—his sound, his smell, the feel of his blonde hair and his skin—those memories try to turn to black and white, and, at times, it's all I can do to hold on to them. With each year that passes, I struggle to hang on to all that was good during his two short years, while everything that was a struggle continues its assault on my life in living color. This section is entitled, *Moving Forward-Learning to Grieve*, but I'm not sure Paige and I could ever really do that.

What we have tried to do is to move to a place where we can be used of God, to allow Him free reign in our lives to use the hurt to glorify Him and help others as they travel a similar path. It's with that thought in mind that I pass on to you this section and tell you how faithful God has been to us every time we have called on Him. I'll include what I have written on various Facebook posts, as well as some other commentary and stories that illustrate how we have grown through the years since our son's death.

One of the first stories I want to pass along is a conversation that took place beside Elijah's casket at Santuck. I wrote earlier that I didn't remember a lot of the folks that came by to pay their respects, but the one that stands out the most is our veterinarian, Doctor Bryson.

CHAPTER 14

I AM NOT ALONE-
OTHERS ARE WITH ME

Romans 12:15 (NIV)
"Rejoice with those who rejoice; mourn with those
who mourn.

I think the worst emotion that grief lays at our door is the feeling that we are alone. And some reading these words may truly be by themselves, having lost their spouse, their child, or their only friend in this life. It is a feeling that I know all too well, and if you've experienced any sort of loss, you likely know it, too. In this chapter, I'll recount several instances when God reminded me that He is with me, holding on to me until I can return His loving embrace in the glory of Heaven.

It was Tuesday, November 25th, 2008. Elijah had passed the previous morning. We had driven to Birmingham to make the arrangements, and we were back within the walls of our church two days before Thanksgiving, with our son in a casket. We started the time of visitation that evening, and before long, there was a line running out of the doors of our church. Paige and I stood there, only a few feet from our lifeless son, and tried our best to put on a smile while we greeted each person who came to pay their respects. Somewhere in the middle of this somber scene, our Veterinarian, Dr. Bryson, had finally reached the two of us.

Dr. Bryson is an older man. At the time of Elijah's passing, he was in his mid-60's. He is a gentle man, of average height and build, with a dry sense of humor. His wife, Beth, is about 14 years his junior, but even with that age gap, they fit each other perfectly. We didn't know them all that well at the time, but we would later become great friends and enjoy their company, going out for pizza at a restaurant in Auburn. Doc, as I call him, is also a very tender man. Although he doesn't wear his emotions on his sleeve, you can still tell that they are there. His attitude and his demeanor fit his profession perfectly.

As Doc stepped up to greet me, I smiled. He didn't smile back; instead, he took my hand with both of his and then pulled me close to him and embraced me. After telling me that he was praying for me, he paused and then spoke words that were a revelation to me.

"I lost my son, too."

My eyes widened, and I spoke to him my condolences, but before accepting them, Doc comforted and taught me a lesson at the same time. He told me that even though he had lost his son, it wasn't the same as what I have been through. Then he told me that I would get through it. The days ahead were going to be hard, but that God would see me through. The pain would always be there, but God's hand was always right behind it, if

I chose to see it.

As he spoke, tears finally began to fall again. The numbness of the situation began to fade, and I realized that he and I were fellow travelers on the same hard road. While I was just at the beginning, he was somewhere in the middle, and he came back, revisited the start of his, just for me. I can't begin to tell you, word for word, what he spoke, but when he moved on to view my son's body, I was comforted...I was encouraged...I had been challenged.

I mentioned earlier that Doc "taught" me that evening. What can anyone learn at their son's viewing? What lessons could possibly be taught at that horrible hour? Many.

For one, I learned that there is great power in not trying to take away someone else's pain, even though you may know a little about it. I also learned that there is equally great power in linking arms with those traveling down roads you have traversed. What Doc did that evening was akin to coming alongside me and pointing my tired and weary eyes back to Jesus. He did that by picking a scab on his own pain and relating to me through the loss of his own son. He relived the terrible days of his own life so that he could bring a little beauty into mine. In short, Doc loved me well that night, and I have not forgotten it.

It's funny that out of all the people who may have shown up that night, I remember very few, and of that number, I remember Doc's visit the best. If you're reading this and you feel alone, I encourage you to seek out those who have gone through the same pain as you. Talk to them and encourage them. Let them encourage you. God works in such ways if we let Him.

CHAPTER 15

I AM NOT ALONE-
OTHERS HAVE COME
BEFORE ME

Hebrews 13:7 (NIV)
"Remember your leaders, who spoke the word of
God to you. Consider the outcome of their way of
life and imitate their faith."

A few months after we buried Elijah, as the emotions that accompany grief were to the point of overwhelming me, God used Brother Larry Gore, once again, to minister to my hurting heart.

I was avoiding the hard conversations with myself because I thought I could outlast the pain. Time heals all wounds, right? It was in one of these self-induced numbing times that God spoke truth into my spirit, once again, and brought me back to the table to face the hurt I was trying to run from.

One Sunday morning, as I was leaving the Sanctuary, Brother Larry pulled me aside. He handed me a piece of paper and told me that it was a poem his grandfather had written years ago. I unfolded the paper and read the handwritten words that had been

I Am Not Alone-Others Have Come Before Me

scribbled down in February of 1937.

It has been four long
years, since you left us
heartbroken and blue.
Just at the time when
our heart was fixed on
the future for you.

But it was God's own
will and plan for you to go
Heaven's glories to you show.

On that dark and chilly
night, when we knew you
had given up the fight.
Oh, how our hearts did ache
But somehow through dark
clouds of sorrow there
God does not make a mistake
But someday on that distant shore
You will be my Harley once more.
for your face to see will be
enough for me.

James Walter Gore
February 7, 1937

Harley died at 16 of an infection from appendicitis. His death was likely slow and painful, and I can relate to the despair Mr. Gore must have felt. After reading it, I handed the piece of paper back to Brother Larry. What

Larry said next stopped me in my tracks and forced me to face my grief head-on.

"My grandfather wrote that four years after Harley passed."

Excuse me? Four years? I realized then that dealing with Elijah's death would never be over. The emotions I was running from would never stop their pursuit of me, and things would never be as they used to. I would never be the same man I was before. Somehow, I had to move forward, knowing that I will carry this burden with me for the rest of my life. I'm not sure I was ready to hear that, but God used Brother Larry to tell me differently.

I thought about that poem and Mr. Gore for the next week or so, and a strange feeling began to come over me. *Comfort.* In a strange way, Mr. Gore's poem let me know that Elijah's memory and life could go on for years and even be used after I'm no longer walking this earth.

Think about it. I didn't know Mr. Gore or Harley, and both were now reunited with Jesus in Heaven and each other. But, Mr. Gore's heartbroken words found their way to my ear. The life of Harley found its way to my ear, and both impacted and changed my life. As the thought of that settled into my heart, I began to accept the fact that Elijah's death would change every part of my life as long as I lived. And that wasn't necessarily a bad thing at all.

***

Another place I have found comfort in the years since Elijah's death is the cemetery. No, I am not referring to where Elijah's earthly body is buried; I am referring to any cemetery in general. Yes, I know how strange that sounds, but bear with me for a few moments and allow me to explain myself.

A few years back, Paige, Maddie, and I were enjoying a Sunday afternoon drive, just exploring different roads we had not yet been down. Think of it as intentionally getting lost. On one of these roads, we spotted an old family cemetery, and I stopped to allow my curiosity to have its fill. No more had we gotten out of the Jeep than we saw the graves of five children all in a row. The last name on the granite markers was Rogers, and their dates were as follows:

Pauline—March 5-25, 1915
O'Dell—January 8-29, 1922
Roberta—May 7-July 14, 1930
Josie—October 6-23, 1932
John—October 6- November 2, 1932

The parents of these children were Mr. and Mrs. J.W. Rogers, and from the little research I have done, they didn't have any children that survived more than a couple of months. What heartache they must have known. Over seventeen years, Mrs. Rogers suffered the loss of five children. Can you imagine?

How in the world does that comfort me? What sick individual would derive comfort from someone else's misery? I'm sure there are those who would ask those questions. Allow me to explain. The part of this that brings me comfort does not reside in the sorrow of these parents. In fact, I grieve with them and understand, somewhat, the feelings they must have had. The part that gives me hope is that Mr. and Mrs. Rogers did not give up. They continued to live life, and they did not let past sorrow dictate their future. If Mrs. Rogers was 20 at the death of her firstborn, Pauline, she would have been 37 at the death of her last two. What does that tell me? She didn't give up on living her life. She didn't give in to the grief, and if she can do it, so can I.

What does that have to do with you and me? Is that just a "don't give up" kind of story? No. I hope that is not all you see. I hope you see that just because you experience one tragic event in your life, that doesn't guarantee you immunity from it ever happening again. That's not how God works. We'll cover that in the next to last chapter, but it bears mentioning here. Because if you are like me, you need to be told more than once. I would imagine that Mrs. Rogers would say the same if she could; don't give up, don't give in. Don't let Satan win your heart by giving in to the grief and sadness. Keep living a God-honoring life; choose to live with a happy heart.

CHAPTER 16

I AM NOT ALONE-GOD IS WITH ME

Psalm 71:16
"I will come and proclaim your mighty acts,
Sovereign Lord; I will proclaim your righteous
deeds, yours alone."

My last story of coming to terms with my grief pertains to the fact that God is always working. He is preparing the healing moments we need years ahead of the actual pain. Let me say that another way. He knew of the tragedies in your life before you ever took a breath, and He has joy available at the exact moment it's needed. This last story is a little different. I wrote the text for my father as a Father's Day present in 2013 shortly after the events it describes. I pray you enjoy it as much as I have.

***

Living by Faith
Written for Philip Partain on Father's Day 2013

You'd think that after almost five years of life in the

"grief process," I would be a little bit wiser in regard to the battles of my mind and more attentive to the warfare of the spirit and heart. If you were to have asked me five years ago where I'd be today, I would have told you without a blink of the eye that healing would've come by now, and Paige and I would be sailing through the placid waters of the joy-filled life. I had no idea that on the day that Elijah left us for eternity, Paige and I were just beginning a lifelong struggle against the enemy's lies and deception. The only combative weapon at our disposal in this conflict is truth. But truth without belief is easily defeated, so it has come down to a matter of belief. Do I really believe God is who He says He is? Are His promises true? These are the questions I found myself facing during a week in April of 2013. Amidst the onslaught of the enemy's lies, I found myself once again in that all too familiar crisis of belief. This is the place where I have a choice, a very simple choice. Do I cry out to God while standing firm in my faith, or do I let my feet search for the footing that cannot be found in the logic of the human mind? This time my heart screamed for God, and His answer to my cry for help still brings tears of joy to my eyes today. It wasn't what I expected, but then again, God doesn't live well in a box no matter how comfortable we try to make it for Him. This story, written for my Dad, is an account of a time when God wouldn't be contained in the cramped condo I had comfortably constructed. Instead, He chose to blow it up and burn the remnants.

This story really starts a few weeks earlier. Paige and I had stopped by the gas station in the Central community to buy a Sunday paper. While looking for a Montgomery paper, my eye spotted an "I Love Eli" T-shirt on the front page of the much smaller Eclectic paper. A quick glance showed our friend Jason Lett's youngest son sporting a hand-me-down shirt that bore my son's name. I thought it was cool, picked up two papers, and after paying for them and the Montgomery paper, I headed out the door. I had no idea that this insignificant event would become the first shot fired in a battle for my mind and heart a little later down life's road.

On a Monday afternoon a few weeks later, I was driving home for lunch from Camp Hill when I heard a familiar song on the radio. I've listened to this song a lot, and the chorus has a line in it that says, *"Who will love me for me? Not for what I have done or what I might become."* On most days, those two sentences wouldn't bother me in the slightest, but this day was different. For reasons I cannot explain or control, my mind was taken prisoner by the thought that I never loved my son for who he was. The demons in my mind ran wild with that thought until I was in tears and screaming on the inside for them to stop. But they didn't. Instead, they took it up a notch, using something meant for good to further infuse my mind with terror, fear, and grief. It was the T-shirts our church sold to help with Eli's medical bills, the same one Keagan Lett was wearing in the picture I saw a few weeks earlier. The demons in my mind told me that Elijah would never be anything more than a name on a T-shirt, and when those wore out, his memory would be thrown away with them, discarded like some piece of trash. In truth, there are times when I have felt like I did give up on Elijah, that I let him go too easily, and that when I should have been fighting for him that I simply laid down like a coward. That rocky ground in my life was the seedbed for these lies that were being flung at me from every direction. During these attacks, I have to rely on truth to come to my rescue. It alone has the power to drive these thoughts and emotions away, but that day was different. No matter how hard I tried to focus on the truth, no matter how hard I prayed, there was no relief. In desperation, I texted my friend Ben Nobles and asked him to pray for me, but to my surprise, I was haunted the rest of the day with the same thought, "You never loved him...His life didn't matter."

As I crawled through that week, the torment eased up a bit, but I felt as if I were walking on eggshells. I was careful about when I listened to the radio and what I read. I purposely avoided anything that had to do with death or children, and I all but quit looking at Facebook for fear of seeing something that might trigger those thoughts again. Every morning during my time with God, I poured my heart out to Him, begging for some bit of truth to be revealed to me as I studied His Word. As the week matured into the weekend, I found myself at an uneasy place. I was balancing in the middle of the seesaw, hoping that no one would jump on either end. On Sunday morning, I gave a passing thought to telling my class about it and asking them to pray for me, but like the coward I feared to be, I relented to teaching the lesson without any mention of the past week's struggle. The rest of the morning was business as usual. I played in the second worship service, listened to the sermon, and played the closing chorus without a peep from God.

I wanted, no, I *needed* something to calm my mind and spirit. As I sat at my drum set rolling up my headphones, I was reminded of something Brother Larry had told me almost five years earlier:

"We are to live by faith and not by sight."

Those are the words he told me one Sunday morning as Paige and I were staggering through Elijah's illness and hospitalization in the fall of 2008. Paige was in the middle of that month and a half-long stretch with him when Brother Larry came up to me one Sunday morning. It was the first Sunday after we learned that Elijah's condition was terminal. He asked me how we were doing; I told him that we were doing ok, that I knew God was going to use this somehow, and that I couldn't wait to see it when He did. That's when, with love, Larry spoke those words to me. At first, I was shocked. How dare he tell me that? If God is going to take my son, shouldn't I at least get to see what He does with it? Don't I deserve that? Of course, I knew he was right, but that didn't change my feelings about it. I wanted to see the work of God, especially if it involved my son, but that's not how God plans things, is it? What God was asking of me was to accept the fact that He would use the illness and death of my son to show Himself to others, even if I wasn't fortunate enough to see it. My sight doesn't validate His work, and even though my heart longed to see what God would do, that wasn't a trade that God was going to make. I had to wait......and believe.

So, with that thought still finding a little traction in the mud of my mind, I finished getting everything organized on my music stand and got up to leave the church. That's when Traci Martin stopped me in front of the pulpit and asked me if I was going to come back for the evening service. After telling her I would, she said that she needed to tell us something, but she had to tell both Paige and me at the same time. Worried instantly, and with a knot in my stomach, I agreed to meet her in the sanctuary at 5:40 that evening. I went home wondering what I had said or done that had gotten me into trouble. I guess that's a holdover from my childhood, because if someone tells me they want to talk to me, my mind tells me I've done something wrong. Of course, it might also have something to do with speaking my mind too often, but that's another story for a later time. At any rate, I spent that afternoon racking my mind for anything I may have said or done to Traci or any member of her family. Ordinarily, that would've ruined my day, but after the past week's torture chamber in my head, this current train of thought was a welcome reprieve.

I must admit that I don't know Traci Martin or her family that well. In a church the size of Santuck, it's hard to get to know many people beyond keeping their name straight. People seem to come and go in your life like the seasons of the year, and while they may still go to church with you, God seems to move friends around each other for particular periods of time. When that time is over, God reshuffles the deck as a new set of challenges are dealt out. As I look back, it amazes me how God has put people in our lives that allowed both couples to bless each other and help us grow spiritually as well. It is a neat dynamic, and only God can get the credit for it. Without Him, these transition periods would be full of turmoil and jealousy, but instead, it is more like the seamless switching of acts in a play. The curtain goes down on one scene and then comes up on another with a new set and cast. And of course, you have the occasional cameo appearance, and that's exactly what God had set up that Sunday afternoon with Traci Martin.

My deacon's meeting was at 3:30 that afternoon, and it was 5:35 when we finished up. I hurried into the sanctuary, where I found Traci sitting with her family on the left side of the church about midway back. Paige joined us shortly thereafter, and Traci led us into the small prayer room in the old vestibule of the church. After we had all sat down in the tiny room, she finally began to speak as the muscles in my stomach tightened. I continued to think about what I may have done wrong, and I tried to still myself and be ready to apologize and ask for forgiveness. This was as uncomfortable as I get. I felt like a schoolboy, taken out into the hall, and waiting for the scolding and paddling to follow. The size of the room didn't help, and it seemed to be an outward expression of how I felt on the inside—tight quarters with nowhere to run. I had no choice but to face the music, but as Traci's words began to find my ears, I quickly realized that it wasn't her talking to me at all. This was a supernatural moment that God had orchestrated, and the more she spoke, the more I realized how perfect God's timing really is.

Traci began by saying, "I don't know how much you know about my past, but I have lived a rough life, so that by my early twenties, I had already had three abortions."

Immediately my mind raced, trying to find a connection between these words and something I must have said to offend her, but there was nothing. I couldn't think of a single thing, but before I could dwell on that thought any longer, she was speaking again. I had to focus, still my mind, and listen to what she said.

She continued. "Because of those abortions, I felt a tremendous amount of guilt and shame, so much so that I could not hold a baby or go anyplace I might be asked to. I avoided all baby showers and nurseries because I couldn't face up to what I had done. I couldn't forgive myself, so I shut everything out and avoided it."

Perplexed and curious, I listened on as she told about all the times in her life this guilt and shame paralyzed her. I felt lost and confused, still wondering what this had to do with me, and why Paige? Why was she here? Then she spoke the words that hushed everything.

"God told me I had to tell you this today."

Now she had my undivided attention. She told us that five years ago, she had gone by our pastor's house to see Brother Gary, but she couldn't remember why. She said that Elijah was there that evening, being kept by Brother Gary and Ms. Jane, and that he was crying uncontrollably when she went inside. With that tidbit of her story, my mind stopped. I knew the night she was talking about, and it was the only time we ever let anyone keep Elijah. It was our anniversary, and since Ms. Jane had been asking us for some time when she could keep him, we finally allowed it so that we could have a couple of hours to ourselves. I never knew that anyone else knew of this until now. She said that as she walked into the living room, they asked her if she wanted to hold him, to see if she could quiet him down. Because of her past, like all the other times she'd been asked this question over the last twenty years, she refused. There was no way she could do it, but Elijah wouldn't stop crying. I knew exactly the cry she was talking about, and I knew the only comfort for him during these times was Paige. She was the chosen one, as far as he was concerned. One moment in her arms and, for him, everything was good again. But Paige wasn't there, and he wouldn't stop crying.

Traci's eyes began to well up, and as hot tears streamed down her cheeks, I handed her a tissue from the table beside me. Looking back up at me, she continued her story as if pressing forward down a path she really didn't want to go down.

"Something inside me told me to hold him that night. Something made me take him in my arms that night."

Now tears began to roll down my face, and Paige's as well.

"When I took him in my arms and held him close to me, he quit crying. He just looked at me, and I looked at him. Twenty years of guilt and shame fell from me, and God started my healing at that moment. I just want you to know that God used your son to change my life."

Was I hearing what my ears told me I was hearing? I was reeling from the words she had spoken, and now a reverent silence filled the room. After a few moments, I finally mustered the voice to speak. I thanked her, hugged her, and tried my best to convey to her what her words meant to us, but before I could leave, God showed off one more time.

Traci reminded me that she works with women at Tutwiler prison in Wetumpka. She councils and ministers to the ladies behind bars for their past, not unlike the prison Traci had constructed for herself in her heart years earlier. As we stood up to leave, Traci said to us that she told Elijah's story to every one of the women she ministers to, and that on the night she tells his story, she wears her "I Love Eli" T-shirt. Again, tears burst from my eyes and ran down my face. Had God really brought this full circle? The very thing that was meant to harm me brought joy to my heart, and a true peace rested in my mind.

A few minutes later, I found myself behind the drum set again, trying to play our evening's worship songs through my giddiness and nervous hands. I could not wait to tell someone—anyone—about how God had just turned my life upside down. I was in awe of His timing and of His perfection. Sure, Traci could have told me that story some five years earlier while I sat behind that same drum set, longing to see how God was using my son. As a matter of fact, she could have told me at any time between then and now, and I would've been deeply moved by her words. But this; this was all God, this was special. God knew the exact moment I needed to hear that, and I would imagine that He was smiling too as He watched me unwrap that gift. And, like a little kid at Christmas, I couldn't wait to show it off. As soon as church was over, I began calling and crying all over again. I couldn't contain it; I didn't want to. I wanted everyone to know what God had done, that He had answered a prayer most unexpectedly, and in the process, showed me what it means to truly live by faith.

CHAPTER 17

A GLASS HOUSE

Psalm 34:18 (NIV)
"The Lord is close to the brokenhearted and saves
those who are crushed in spirit."

This next chapter contains different Facebook posts that I have written over the years since Elijah passed. Like waves in the ocean, grief often comes in tides and varies with the seasons of the year. Most of these posts were written in the fall of the year when the waves usually grow fierce and rough. I hope that you'll see the unpredictability in these writings as they give an account of the passing of the years without my son. As always, just as Doc told me, God's graceful hand of mercy is there if we will but ask for it.

August 19, 2009

It was late December the last time I wrote about anything regarding Elijah. I have purposely kept my feelings silent, and I have tried not to comment much on how Paige, Maddie, and myself are coping with this. But, after a lot of encouragement from a few friends, I have decided to break my silence and write again. This is not something I write to gain any attention for myself or to bring notice to a situation that most people feel is bad enough already. It is something that I do for those out there who want to know. Those who care for us enough to want to know how to pray. How to pray, you ask? Yes, it's when "Bless them, Lord" isn't enough anymore. It's when you pray for someone so intently and for so long that their cares, concerns, and hurts feel as painful as your own. It is for those few people that this is written. Not for the spiritual rubberneckers that just want to see enough of the pain to feel better about themselves or the ones who callously dismiss my son's death by saying things that should be kept to themselves. No, this is not for them. Not at all.

With that said, I find myself in the position I like the least: that of a transparent Christian. I do not like wearing my innermost feelings on the outside for all to see. Instead, I prefer to put them in a closet deep into the recesses of my heart. They are safe there. No one knows of them, and no one can see them. I have hidden them so well that even I have trouble finding them. I like it that way. It seems to be easy, but like all easy routes in life, it turns out to be hard. Sooner or later, the closet must be cleaned out. It cannot hold anymore and must be gone through piece by piece. That's the hard part. That's this part. So, let's get with it. Let's start the cleaning. It's time for a yard sale.

Elijah was my second child and my only son. When I think of him, I have bittersweet memories that come and go like lightning flashes in my mind. I can think of his sweet smile, and before that memory can settle on my mind, another flash of lightning displays his pale, sick body, deprived of nourishment, struggling for the next breath that never comes. I can think of his homecoming from the hospital five months after he was born, but that memory is replaced with the homecoming 18 months later with hospice and a terminal illness. In short, I can think of all the happy times in his life when everything was as it should be, but they are only to be replaced with the memories that no one wants. Those are the memories that keep you up at night. They are the ones that do their wicked work in your heart night after night. The memories that seem to be all evil, dancing in your head like the savages they are. I find myself in that terrible storm of thoughts more often than I want to share, and I would imagine that, left unchecked, it would certainly get out of hand. What would come of it? Depression? Anxiety? Better yet, what takes them away? Time? Counseling? I have found only one way to clear my head of them. One Way to have peace in the midst of those bolts of terror. His name is Jesus. I simply ask Jesus to take them away, and just as He did two thousand years ago in an old fishing boat, He does in my storm-tossed mind. He says, "Peace, be still," and they are gone. What a simple thing! What a wonderful thing! Gone are the thoughts of my son's struggles, his terrible pain, and his all too short life. They are replaced by the knowledge that he is with Jesus, SEEing Jesus, worshiping the Father, and waiting on me.

Now all of that sounds good, doesn't it? Walking with Jesus every day, letting Him have all my worries and cares, and just living it up spiritually, right? Sounds easy enough, but unfortunately, it's really hard. For some reason, it seems better to hold on to the pain that Elijah's death has caused without living in the victory that Jesus has won. Why do I struggle with this? I guess it's because in my flesh, I want to be in control. I want to do it. What happens on those days? Well, it's a nightmare. The storms in my mind rage out of control until I can take it no longer. Just like those weary disciples in that fishing boat, I have to wake up Jesus. Do you think that when Jesus went to sleep on the boat that He had a smile? He knew what was coming, and He knew the answer. Like the disciples, I take my eyes off of Him. I tell Him to take a nap so that I can have a turn at the helm. How does that turn out? You know. I know it too. But why can't I see that every day? Every moment? Why must I wait until the boat is almost sunk before going to the Man who can walk on water? Does it make sense? It doesn't to me either, but none of this makes sense at times. I still have questions about it. I have a lot of "whys" that I would love to ask God, but do I ask them? Sometimes I do. The answers vary. Sometimes there isn't one, but most times, there are. Usually, I have to answer the question, "Do you trust Me?" Do I? I mean, do I really trust God? Of course. But do I trust Him with everything? With my life, Paige, my children? Do I really? If I do, then why question The Creator? He is sovereign. He is just. I have to realize that Elijah was my earthly son, but he is God's property. For that matter, I am too. So is Paige and anyone else that claims to be a Christian. Looking at it that way, I have to understand that I can only praise God for allowing me the time that I did have with Elijah. He was entrusted to me for a season, and for reasons I cannot explain, nor do I need to understand, he was taken back.

So, if you want to know where I am, this is it. I am striving each day to see Jesus through my grief, to fellowship with Him, and let Him comfort me in a way that only He can.

It's easy for me to read this and see that Paige and I were in the birth pangs of grief and loss. I look back and see that I was trying to come to terms with Elijah's death in a way that supported my "grin and bear it" Christianity. I was doing a poor job of it, and my emotions were battling with my faith. I knew enough to look to God for the answers to the questions I posed, but like Job in his grief, I'm not sure I had a good grasp of the true nature of the One I worshipped. I didn't know it when I wrote this, but the ash pile of Job was going to get a lot deeper before I found my way off it.

I also see anger in that first paragraph. I was beginning to distance myself and my family from great people like Jonathan and Christy Stuart, people who had walked hand in hand with us from the beginning of Elijah's life until the end. Here I was, an angry person who had no idea how to cope with what I was feeling and taking my misery out on those who loved me. I would eventually begin to right this ugly wrong, and to the Stuart's credit, they were willing to forgive and love this repentant sinner as if I had never hurt them.

If you're reading this and you see the seeds of anger begin to sprout against those you love, I have one word for you: STOP! People do not know what to say or do in these situations, so don't hold them responsible for any perceived shortcomings. It's more likely than not that it's simply your perception of what may have been said or done. If anger must be expressed, I'll tell you something that might shock you; express that anger to God. He alone has the shoulders big enough to take it, and He sees something that no one else can, including yourself. He sees your heart. He knows how you feel and created the emotions you're feeling. Take it to Him. Hold Him responsible and ask Him the hard questions. But be ready, like our friend Job, to hear answers you might not be ready for.

October 7th, 2009
I didn't realize why Elijah was so heavy on my heart this morning until I realized that it was one year ago today that he went into the hospital for the last time. Praise God he doesn't have to endure this life any longer! He is perfect now.

Like the day I described as I began this book, thoughts and memories flood a grieving soul with no warning. I think this post was likely a warning shot of the Octobers to come. From this first one in 2009 until this writing, I know that at some point in October, I will be reminded of and begin to relive my son's life. The moments can be hard, and the tides of sadness can threaten to flood my soul, but I have learned that I decide who and what I allow into my heart. Some days that simple thought is enough, and I remind myself to lock out the unwanted intruders that lie and steal, but in fact, there are other days during those few months that I leave the door of my heart wide open, and I find my soul robbed of any joy.

Perhaps you're reading this and understanding the analogy I'm using. Maybe you're at your wit's end, struggling through a time when you're reminded of every hurt and failure life has brought to your doorstep. The only advice I have is to look to God's Word and let Him lock the door. Let Him sing His song of truth in your heart. You are valuable to Him, and He sees every single tear that falls from your eyes.

November 6, 2009

Happy Birthday, Elijah! I love you and miss you so much. There is no poetry, no song in my heart. It is still broken, and it longs to see you again. But my Joy will come in the morning, and He will wipe away all my tears. Until then, my son, until then.

It had been almost a year, and it felt like everyone else had moved on. Some folks, with good intentions, did not understand that post. I played golf with a guy from church shortly after this, and he made fun of the language I had used. I smiled as he talked about how his wife related to it and cried over it as it touched her heart. It may not have impacted him very much, but even through his callousness, I saw a clear way to keep my son's memory alive— by writing about the hardest parts of it and baring my soul to people I didn't even know.

November 24, 2009

It has been a year since The Lord took Elijah home, so I thought I would write a note about it. And as most of you know, Paige also uses my Facebook page to keep up with every one of you too. She will not create her own page, but I really don't mind sharing this with her. If I did, I sure wouldn't tell her. Anyway, to my surprise, and yours as well, she has also written a note. I cannot tell you what it means for me to see her finally open up a little about this. I won't say anymore, I can't, I'll just let you read like I did.

Paige's Note:

Matt has told me many times that everyone asks how I am really doing. The truth is that even Matt does not know. I keep pretty much everything to myself. To say that the year since Elijah and Mom's death has been difficult is an understatement. Many of you know that my mom was my best friend, and I talked to her at least twice a day. It has been very hard for me not to be able to call her in times of need. I thought that it would get easier, but to me, it just gets harder and harder each day. It is hard when you have found a true joy and meaning to your life, and for me, that was to care for Elijah, a special needs child. No one wants their child to be anything but healthy, but God had different plans for him. Elijah was born with many difficulties to overcome. He was blind, developmentally delayed, and had other problems, but through all of this, I found that he was the greatest blessing to me. He loved to hear my voice, and when he heard it, he would give the biggest grin. He brought joy to me even though he was not going to be a normal child. He taught me a lot about life and how other people see and treat a child that is different. It is just so hard getting up every day knowing that you are supposed to be able to go into your child's bedroom and see their face, smile, and love, but the reality is that one door is always closed. It is just too hard to face the pain that he will never be in there again.

Now, the reality is that I have only one room to go into, and she is the love of my life. She is the reason I keep going. I still have one miracle to help me: Maddie Grace. She is such a joy and inspiration for me to keep going day to day. There are many days that I do not want to get out of bed, face people, or talk to anyone. But she deserves to have the best of me, so she keeps me going. She seems to understand and reason all the hurt better than I do. It is just hard to do the normal things I used to. Just seeing a little baby boy or other things reminds me of what life used to be like. It is hard to get people to be thankful for the family in their life, but when something happens to two of the most important people in your life, you learn to love and enjoy every second with those you still have here.

I want to spend every minute with Matt and Maddie and just let them know how much I love them and what they mean to me. Many people say that we know Elijah is better off in heaven. That may be true, but it is not your child or your life that has been changed. I still miss him more than I ever have. God is the only reason that I can keep going with so much hurt. He is the only One who makes that possible. Every day is a new battle, but I know that God has a plan for all of the hurt I am going through. One day I will understand it all. When I see my Father face to face, I will understand all this pain and sorrow.

I have come to understand that God never promises a life free from pain.

"The presence of hardship in your life does not imply the absence of God. Use these circumstances to find God. He desires for you to understand His purpose for allowing these difficulties in your life."

Elijah and Mother, this time a year ago, I watched both of you become angels. I love you, and I can only pray that I have shown the love and grace of our Lord through this difficult situation.

Matt's note:

When I was a little boy, I looked forward to the month of November all year long. November was my birthday month (19th), but it also started the Christmas season. I looked forward to the sight of the Sears Christmas wish book and the smell of Momma baking a chocolate cake for my birthday. November seemed to keep the promises of what may lie ahead. Maybe some new clothes for Christmas? Maybe something bigger or better? Some of those years when Dad was out of a job, Christmas wasn't much more than a Hot Wheels or two, and even once, Jeff and I got some IOUs. No kidding.

As I got older and other things of my childhood faded, November remained just as special as ever. I asked Paige to marry me on November 9th, 1997, and both of our children were born in this seemingly magical month, Maddie on the 2nd in '04 and Elijah on the 6th in 2006. Adding to that, Thanksgiving has always been one of the most special times for me. My family would get together and feast on turkey, dressing, ham, cranberry sauce, and lots more. The meal would be crowned with a chocolate cream pie, and I would be in pain from the excess. More important than the food was the time with my family. Even when I was in the Navy, I tried to make it home for every Thanksgiving. Out of four, I missed one. Although I called at 2:00 AM (my time) and spent $10 for 10 minutes on the sailor phone, it was worth it just so I could feel like I was there for a minute with my family.

Indeed, I have always been a family man. I have always been one to love and cherish the time spent with them. Those times and memories are more precious than anything this world has to offer. No amount of money or gold would entice me to give them up. They are sacred to me. But last November wasn't as kind as my previous 32. No, last November would seem to be a month worth forgetting. In that month, we said goodbye to Paige's mother, Donna, and to our son, Elijah. There were no birthday parties like most years, no wonderful celebrations with laughter floating through the air like the scent of a pumpkin pie. Last year was different. It was a time of mourning and of loss. It was a time when we, as a family, watched two people who we loved with all our heart slowly fade away. It wasn't like a sudden disaster or an unexpected tragedy. This was slow and deliberate. When looking at it, you could almost say that there isn't one thing that I should be thankful for during that terrible month. I would have every right to lock myself up inside a black room, letting no one in, and feel sorry for myself, and the way last November treated me, I could do that. I would be within my rights, wouldn't I? After all, one year ago today, my son took his last breath. Doesn't that justify it? Well, let's look at it this way and see.

One year ago today, my son opened his eyes into a glorious majesty I cannot imagine. He walked for the first time down golden streets, hearing multitudes of angels sing the Lord's praise. I would imagine that he ran to Jesus and traced out the holes in His hands, the hands that help pay the price for his admission into that beautiful place. He finally saw his Maw Maw, Pa Pa Bailey, Grandpaw Partain, and all the others who he had heard about. I imagine that he fell to his knees the instant he saw the Father and worshiped the God that gave me the precious two years that I had with him. Can you see it? I can. I can see that God has given my son everything I could not. He has given him sight, the ability to walk, a perfect home, and above all else, He has given him a perfect love. As much as I love Elijah, I couldn't give him what he has now...an eternity with Jesus. I couldn't pay that price. I am not worthy.

So, what do you think? Should I lock myself up in that black room, or should I be thankful for everything Elijah now has and one day I'll have too? With this in mind, the question becomes this. How can I not be thankful? How could I say that I will choose to go to that dark place when my son is with The Light? Elijah is there...right now.

So, I will choose today, a year since my son died, to praise God with all my heart. To thank Him for the son He gave me and for The Son He gave for me. I will thank Him for the beautiful memories I have of Elijah, yes, even of last November. Although I can still see his pained, frail body in my mind, I will choose to see God allowing some time for us to say goodbye. I will choose to see that God's plan is perfect and His will is not flawed. I will choose to thank God for Elijah and thank Him for paying the price that I could not. And, I will end that prayer of thankfulness as I have ended every prayer since then...."God, please tell my son that I love him."

Paige's words were more than I could handle, and truth be told, they still bring water to my eyes today. She does not show her emotions easily, and, as you'll read in another post, the times that I have been allowed to peer into her broken heart, I have seen a beautiful picture of God's grace and mercy.

In my words, I see a father trying to make sense

of what he's feeling. I'm still trying to put a bow on the whole ordeal, and I'm looking for a way to weave this beautiful picture together. I knew I had a choice on what my thoughts were, but, if I'm honest, I'm not sure I had really experienced the full spectrum of emotions yet. That was coming, but so was God's gentle hand.

November 6, 2010

Four years ago today, my life was changed when my son was born at almost 25 weeks. In the following two years, I learned more about God and myself than in my previous 31. I can safely say that given the opportunity, I would go through every bit of it all over again.

November 24, 2010

We all miss our little Angel, Chief, and Bubba so much. It has been 2 years since we last got to see him. It is just as hard today as it was 2 years ago. I just want to hold my little man, but I know that he is happy in heaven with Jesus and his Maw Maw. Just want to be thankful for the 2 years we had with him. What a blessing he was to us. We learned more in that 2 years than we ever have.

Love Daddy, Mommy, and Sister

I wrote the first post on his birthday, and Paige took the time to write the second one on the anniversary of his death. We both wrote of "learning" during his two years on this earth. Granted, this was not an elective course, but one that we were forced to take. But even today, almost twelve years after his death, I wouldn't take anything for those precious two years.

November 6, 2011

It's hard to believe that today is Elijah's 5th birthday and that the 24th of this month will mark his 3rd year in heaven. It makes me stop to wonder what might have been, but also look back at how blessed we have been as a family. Although part of my heart went to heaven with Elijah 3 years ago, that will never overshadow the blessing that he was for the 2 years he was here. Happy Birthday, my son. You will always be my little Chief.

Matt

November 6, 2011

Today is my sweet angel's 5th birthday!!! I miss him so much. He was my life for 2 years. I know heaven got a special blessing, but it is still just as hard. I love you, little angel. Happy Birthday love, Mom and Sister. You will always be my little angel and Maddie's little Bubba.

Love you, Mom.

Somewhere around this time, two things started occupying my thoughts. The first was the fact that Elijah had now been gone longer than he lived. I started fearing that I would somehow forget him. That thought makes me laugh today, but it was very real then, and I can see in my words a recollection of sorts.

Grief is a very strange animal. At times it can be a beast, ready to devour you, with no escape from its sharp claws. Other times it is a pet of comfort in your lap, reminding you of all that is right in your life. Quite the paradox, but no less true.

The second thought that penetrated my conscience was how we would honor Elijah's memory on a permanent basis. Others who had lost children set up scholarships in their name, held benefits for hospitals, and put their child's name on the lips of everyone in the community. How could we do that? I wanted everyone to know my son's name, and I wanted to see lives changed because of it. That felt only natural. But my mind could never rest with any of those thoughts. Perhaps because it was too much akin to my unrealistic dreams for Elijah in the beginning. Was it not enough that my life was changed? Maybe that's where I needed to start. Could it be that all I needed to do to honor my son's memory, and his all too short life, was to live mine to the fullest?

April 22, 2012

For the past several years, after I finished playing in each service at church, I have gone down to the nursery to check on the babies before I go to Sunday School or worship. It's a habit I started after Elijah was born because I wanted to make sure that he was ok. Even after he passed, I continued to do it because I could think about seeing him in that familiar place and imagine hearing his sound again. But, after a long talk with a good friend, I have realized that the few minutes I spent down there after the first service was cutting into the short time I had to teach Sunday School. So today I changed it. I gave it up because I know that those few minutes could be the difference in someone's life in my class. Even though it's been almost 4 years since Elijah left us, I am still learning that I must find ways to move on. It seems as time goes on, I have a choice to make. I can either use his death as a crutch or a catalyst. It can teach me things that I never would have understood before, like the fact that life is precious and that maybe the life I need to be worried about is sitting in my class waiting on me on Sunday morning.

The friend in this post is Ben Nobles, who, at that time, was one of our Associate Pastors. He came to our church a few months before Elijah passed, and he and I grew very close during that time.

I found myself trying to hold on to Elijah's memory by continuing in the ruts and routines that I wore into the fabric of my life while he was here. After talking with Ben, I realized that I could honor my son's life best by living my own. I could strive to be the man I dreamed he would become, and I could allow God free reign to use every part of my life, including the hurts I still carried.

You see, grief has a way of leading us away from living life. It took almost four years for me to see it, but once I felt free to live again, I started looking for ways to use Elijah's memory to help others. I no longer kept my struggle to accept my son while he was here a secret, and as I embraced the past, I felt liberated to live in the present. Make no mistake, however; allowing God free reign to use every part of my life meant that I had to give up any sort of fake "I have it all together" Christianity. I was beginning to understand that allowing God to use this part of my life meant that I had to be comfortable exposing it. That, my friend, is never easy, but I have found no greater peace than when I acknowledge my brokenness.

June 24, 2012
Isn't it funny how that one thing you thought you never wanted to happen a few years ago is the one thing

that you would give anything for today? I was reminded of it yet again this morning as we ate our breakfast at the hotel before checking out. At the next table was a family of four with two sons. One of them was a special needs child in a wheelchair and had trouble talking and eating. They were patient with him, listening intently to every word, emotion, and feeling he tried to convey. His irregular movements and broken speech weren't a bother to them. They weren't ashamed or embarrassed. It was in that moment, with tears in my eyes, that I realized just how many times I had prayed against the life they now enjoyed. As much as I wanted my son to be normal this time four years ago, I would give anything—ANYTHING—to have been able to sit down at a table this morning and have him by my side. So, I had to excuse myself, as I often do in these situations, to go and find a quiet place to pray. Be careful what you consider troublesome in your life. Those things that you think are holding you down may just be the things holding you up higher than you thought.

We had traveled to Greenville, South Carolina, to watch the Lion King musical at the Peace Center for Paige's birthday. I was still trying to figure out what using Elijah's memory to move forward would look like in my life. That morning, in the hotel's breakfast area, I could feel something in me stirring as I watched the scene I described in that post.

This was not the first time something like this had happened. In truth, there are not many places we go to that I don't see something or someone that reminds me of Elijah and my struggle to accept him. What was different this time was that after I shared this, after I admitted the elephant in the room was there, there was a peace in my heart. It was like I could write out my grief and sorrow, setting it free for all the world to see.

It's difficult to explain but allowing myself to be made small sure helped me put God in His proper place. This journey was no longer about me but about my God and His wonderful grace and mercy. I can only pray that whoever may have read my words would take them to heart and love their children for who God made them to be. Going forward, I finally saw an avenue in my grief that God could use, but it looked nothing like I had originally envisioned. In fact, I would need to grow even more comfortable with being uncomfortable.

November 6, 2012

This morning six years ago, I had no way of knowing that by the end of the day, my life would be upside down, and I would be begging God to save the lives of my wife and newborn son. No way of knowing that within the next few hours, all the stability I thought I enjoyed would be shaken. But that's exactly what happened. We rarely know when the moments that truly shape us are coming, and that day was no exception for me. At 9:27, I answered my cell phone. As soon as I heard Paige's voice, I knew what was wrong. Like it or not, she was giving birth to our son, almost 4 months early, at home. Within the next 35 minutes, as I drove as fast as possible, our home became the scene out of some Hollywood movie. Sheriff's Deputies, church friends, ambulances, and medics were everywhere. When I arrived, I ran upstairs to Elijah's delivery room, our bathroom, to try and comfort Paige. The first time I saw Elijah, he was nothing more than a small figure on our bed surrounded by the people working desperately to save his life. I gave up on their effort shortly after he was loaded onto the helicopter in our pasture. I assumed he wouldn't make it, but I was wrong. God surprised us that day, this day six years ago, and I will celebrate that surprise as best I can. Sure, it would easy to focus on the grief of losing him two years later, but I've faced that monster, and it's not a path I'm going to take today. Today I will choose to look at his short life and the miraculous way it began. I will stand on the promises of my God, and I will thank Him for the joy my son brought to me and everyone else who knew him. Because, after all, the joy of having him will always outweigh the grief of losing him. Happy Birthday, my son. You will always be my little Chief.

More admissions to giving up and giving in when I felt I should have stood strong, but this admission was different. I was finally finding the path that I had been looking for, a way to honor and remember my son ensuring that his memory was kept alive.

I also began to recognize that I still had a choice in my grief. I didn't have to feel beat up and depressed every time I thought about my son. Sure, I could still feel sadness—that's a God-given emotion—but there could be a joy that followed if I chose to find it. I could either wallow in self-pity, or I could choose to live in the joy of the moment. I asked myself what Elijah would want me to do? That answer was easy. I just needed to accept it.

November 24, 2012

This morning four years ago, I placed my hand on my son's back, and I felt his chest rise and fall for the last time. I was fortunate enough to be there for the moment when he finally let go of this world and entered into an eternity with Jesus. Now, if you have read any of my previous posts from this month, you have gotten an idea of what the month of November is like around our home. It is one emotional event right after the other. It seems to hit a crescendo today, the anniversary of Elijah's death. Some may think that I write about these events to gain attention for some pity party we are throwing each November as we wallow in our grief and anxiety, but nothing could be farther from the truth. I write to let others know that even though life knocked us down, God has raised us up. He has been and continues to be our strength and our hope and has led us through the most difficult times that anyone could imagine. We know that even though He allowed our son and Paige's mother to be taken from us four years ago, He did not leave us here to live a life of death and suffering but has filled the void of death with blessings and victory. Today we do not hang our heads in defeat and think about what has been taken from us, but instead, we lift our hands in praise and acknowledge what God has given us. I cannot think of a better way to honor my son and his memory. And if today he can look down from heaven, I want him to see his father thanking God for his life and not living in the darkness of the past. I want Elijah to finally see in eternity what he felt on this earth; that his parents love him with all of our hearts, and we strive to honor God with every moment of our lives.

It had been four years since we buried our son, and I was starting to understand that walking down the road of grief is like being stuck in the Alabama mud. Sometimes you're just spinning your wheels, not going anywhere, stuck right where you don't want to be. Finally, you begin to move, and you think you're free of the trap, only to stop once again, wheels spinning furiously but going nowhere. At some point, you hope to get out of the hole you're in, but until conditions change, all you do is mash the gas pedal of life and live.

That's where I found myself four years down this road. I felt like we were finally moving again, but I wasn't sure how long the momentum would last. It didn't take long before God put a young man in my life that pulled the makeshift bandage off my heart and stuck me right back in the mud. The mere sight of him would force me to see my life differently and would walk me back down a path I thought I'd left behind, in a place I last saw my son's face.

> June 21.2013
>
> Enjoying the evening with my parents, aunt and uncle, and a special little boy. Keith and Rebecca Ray, I know you already know this, but every time I see your son God uses him to bless me. It is pure joy to see the young man he's becoming (with that devious smile), and I hope you don't mind if, from time to time, I look at him and catch a glimpse of what might have been.

I first heard of Jonathan Ray when he was two years old, sometime between 2009-2010. His dad, Keith, was my father-in-law's Pastor at Bold Springs Presbyterian Church at the time, and Paige's grandmother and father talked about how Jonathan looked like Elijah. I didn't take what they were saying to heart too much until I finally saw the young man in the sanctuary of Bold Springs one Sunday.

Like Elijah, Jonathan was born very early and spent a long time in the NICU. He also has blonde hair, and his frame, as well as his face, were almost identical to my son's. One look at him that day, and I had to leave the sanctuary. I walked down to my son's grave, barely able to see through the tears that couldn't be held back.

I stood there in front of the granite teddy bear that bears my son's name and the dates of his birth and death and asked God, why? Why would You do this to me? Why here? In that first difficult moment, it felt as if God was rubbing my nose in the failure I had always feared to be. So, I stood there, jaw clenched tight, shaking my head, and accusing God of the torment in my mind and heart.

The anger felt justified until I looked again at Elijah's headstone. The teddy bear hiding behind the heart seemed to be looking at me, questioning why I was so angry. As I returned the lifeless bear's gaze, I thought about the choice I now had. Sure, I could see this young boy, and I could be reminded of the failure I feared to be. Or, I could look upon what appeared to be the face of my son, and I could get a small glimpse of Elijah.

With that newfound perspective, I dried my eyes, asked God to forgive me, thanked Him for the privilege of seeing a young man like Elijah, and walked back in with a grateful heart.

I found Jonathan again, in the arms of his mother, and a genuine smile crept across my face. I allowed my mind and heart to imagine a little, to dream a dream I hadn't dreamed in a very long time.

A year or two later, when this post was written, Keith was my parent's Pastor, and we had the privilege of keeping Jonathan one evening while his parents took some time for themselves. What an evening that was! To have a few hours to relive and redo meant more than anything. It was a blessing I am inadequate to put into words.

Nov 6.2013

Happy 7th Birthday, Elijah! It sure doesn't seem like you should be seven already or that you've been waiting on us for almost 5 years. Where has the time gone? It seems like only yesterday that we celebrated the joy of bringing you home from the hospital, and only a few hours since we celebrated your eternal homegoing to Heaven. That makes me wonder what you've been doing up there, how beautiful it is, and if you care to look over the edge of that wonderful place to catch a glimpse of us down here. I like to imagine you laughing and smiling in the arms of your Maw Maw as the light of Jesus fills every corner and crevice of that majestic place. And angels singing? How amazing does that sound? Have you seen my Grandpaws yet? They were both good men. They were the kind of man I always thought you'd grow into and the kind of man I hope to be. That brings me to my next question. Have I made you proud? I know it took me a while to finally accept the fact that you'd never be the boy I had dreamed of before you were born, but I hope Jesus told you that you were far more than I could have ever imagined. You did more in the two years you were here than I could've thought, and you touched so many people. I'm still finding out the ways that God used you to change people's lives. You wouldn't believe the story I was told just this past April. A lady said to me that God used you to heal the hurts that she had carried for over twenty years. All I could do was cry at the thought of it. I still see you at times. God has placed a few little boys in my life that remind me of you, and there is this one boy who looks identical to you. He could pass for your twin. It sure was hard the first time I saw him, but now I look at him and see a blessing from God. Has Jesus been giving you the messages I've sent? Whenever I talk to Him, I always ask Him to tell you how much I love you. I hope you know that even though I love you that much, I still wouldn't bring you back if I had the chance. Nope. I would leave you there in the perfection of Heaven, in the midst of angels, and in the presence of God. A boy like you deserves a place like that, and even though the hurt is unbearable at times, your Mom and I will be ok until Jesus calls us home, too. I know that we will be fine because Jesus told me that He would never leave us. He is with us, living in us, and He is with you, so I guess that means that we're not really that far apart after all. It is on days like today that I daydream about the moment when we will see you again. I know it will be more wonderful than words can describe, and my heart will finally be made whole again. Happy Birthday, my dear son. I love and miss you so much.

I took a different approach this year. I felt the need to write an open letter to my son. Even though I posted it, I wrote it for myself. The peace I felt afterward was indescribable.

Nov 24, 2013

Well, today marks the start of another year without Elijah. It doesn't seem like it, but it has been 5 years since he went home to be with Jesus. Maddie held him that morning as Paige and I knelt beside our bed and said a prayer over his lifeless body. Both of us thanked God for His love, mercy, and the life of our son. At that moment, we began the rest of our lives knelt down in praise to our Father instead of hobbled by a godless sorrow. Two days later, in the sanctuary at Bold Springs Church, we sealed his casket with our kisses and said our final good-byes. I was sure I would never see him again on this earth, but I could have never guessed what gifts the grace of God would give me over the next five years. A year later, in the same sanctuary where I last saw my son, God allowed me to see a boy almost identical to Elijah. He used that boy, Jonathan Ray, to start perpetual healing in my heart that continues to this day. Before that day, I thought that I would never again experience the joy only the father of a son knows. To be able to see him grow and become a man, to watch him tackle the hard things in life with determination, and to guide him in his life as he comes to know the nature of God through my example. All those wonders were lost to me until that day, and God used little Jonathan to open my eyes. Elijah was only dead if I allowed him to die in my heart. I could still see him if I wanted, and more importantly, I could still be the father I dreamed of being if I chose to. So, after that day, I began to see "glimpses," as I call them. I could see Elijah in the lives of others and rekindle the fire of being a father to a son. Before I knew it, I could see him everywhere. In a young boy named Zek,

I could see the bond with his mother like Elijah had with Paige. Another boy named Justice showed me Elijah's determination through the hardships of life. Yet, another displayed the love for Maddie that Elijah had. His name is Zach. The list of names could go on and on, but you get the idea. I have learned during this time that we are never too broken to be used of God; and that He loves us through every hard moment of our lives. His blessings are there if we choose to see them, and His grace will always outweigh our grief no matter how dark the day might seem. If we are His children, then we are never far apart from those who have gone on before us, and we have that blessed hope of seeing them again. Until that wonderful day, I will continue to look for Elijah in any place he might be hiding; because I never know the blessing of a "glimpse" that's right around the next corner.

I love the little "glimpses" I get, and yes, even today, they still come. I'm not sure I'll ever outgrow looking for him in the lives of others, especially children. I have found that my heart feels the most complete when around other children. I don't know why, but it may be because there's always the chance that I'll catch a "glimpse" of my son.

Jan 8, 2014

"Give it over to God." "Let God handle it." I have heard those two phrases and repeated them more often than I can count, but I have found that the application of them is where it gets difficult. I was reminded of that again last night and this morning when Maddie started complaining of a little discomfort in her stomach and chest. Nothing major, but you could tell she wasn't feeling 100%. "Here we go again," I thought as I tucked her in, and we said our nighttime prayers.

It seems like I have been waiting for the other shoe to drop ever since we lost Elijah. Before you start laughing at me, I'll remind you that there was that first day with him. What I mean by that is for every one of us who has been through something terrible, there was always the start of it. You know, day one? The day when the situation you thought was a minor inconvenience revealed itself for the monster it truly was. In our case, it was an ordinary trip to the doctor because Elijah was more fussy than normal. Forty-five days in the hospital, two months, and six surgeries later, he took his final breath, and I was left wondering when, not if, the next tragedy was going to strike. Paige's almost yearlong hospital stay in 2012 did nothing to quench that occasional feeling either.

So, I hope you can understand why something as simple as a tummy ache in my 9-year-old daughter can trigger painful emotions and questions about my faith and the nature of God. With that said, let's reconsider those two phrases. What does it really mean to "give it over to God" or to "let God handle it"? I think it means that we, or at least I, must live in a constant state of submission to Him with every moment of my day placed at His feet. I must believe, not just understand, that God is sovereign and that He alone is in control of my life and the lives of those I love. He knows my heart, which means that He knows my pain, hopes, dreams, and whatever else crosses my often-bewildered mind. And, I must do this with every new thought. 2 Corinthians speaks of "taking every thought captive." I believe that's what I have to do so that I will not live in the past and relive all of those painful memories over something as minor as a tummy ache. Yes, it could be day one, but if it is, then I believe God is already there on the last day of it, and He's there with me every day in between. Maybe that's how we give it over to Him, but I'm starting to think that He's got it all along. It's just up to me to see it that way.

Yeah, I wish I could say that this post described the only time I struggled with this "other shoe dropping" feeling, but I'm not going to lie. This battle is never over in my mind, but I have learned that the only way I can fight this battle is on my knees before God. I can't do it on my own.

I know that life ends in death and that, as a believer, I have a hope that is more beautiful than the death that ushers us into it. When I struggle, I have taken my mind off of that hope, and I grow nearsighted in seeing the physical instead of the spiritual. I would guess that this battle will not be over until I am no longer in this world but it should never keep me from knowing that the war has been won.

Aug 3, 2014

I have been told that when you receive a gift from God, the only way to keep it is to give it away. That sounds strange to me, but if you take the time to let that thought marinate a little, it starts to make sense. So, if you'll pardon this long post, I'll give away the gift I received this evening at our church's community celebration.

This event is kind of like a fair with different booths representing the various ministries of our church, and it is a way of showing our community who we are as one part of the body of Christ. There were all kinds of other community organizations there as well, including the new Haynes helicopter ambulance. For those that don't know, our son Elijah was airlifted from our home the day he was born, so the sound or sight of one of those aircraft brings back vivid memories of that day. It draws Paige and me right back into the struggle his life was and can serve as a reminder of all that we feel like we've lost. So, like a moth to a flame, I wanted to watch this thing take off, knowing full well what might happen.

As the pilot started the engine and the rotors began to spin, I felt a knot form in my stomach. A few seconds later, the helicopter lifted off of the ground and sped off into the blue sky. As I watched it leave, I felt the feelings I have tried so hard to bury begin to rise back up into my heart. After I had found Paige, I saw that she was having the same reaction I was. From behind her sunglasses, tears began to fall, and as we embraced, I felt the anger start to well up within me. The lies that are so easy to believe began to run through my mind, and as an old friend consoled Paige, I sat in my chair, trying hard to focus on the truth. I told myself that his two years were not wasted; I knew people whose lives were changed, and that should have been enough. Sadly, at that moment, it wasn't. Then I saw it. A young boy, Jacob Callen, was wearing one of the "I Love Eli" shirts sold by our church when we were coming to the close of Elijah's time on this earth. Jacob has the smile of an angel and wears his shirt more than anyone else who may have bought one almost 6 years ago. But even at that, I doubt he could've known that by wearing one tonight, he would be used of God to help patch up a breaking heart. You see the verse on the back of that shirt is Philippians 1:6: "Being confident of this, that He who began a good work in you will carry it on to completion until the day of Christ Jesus." Reading that verse from his back this evening reminded me that the "good work" God has begun in me is far from over, even though Elijah's work has been completed. That shirt also reminded me that I was surrounded by those who have been through this struggle with us. They hurt when we did, celebrated when we did and bore the burden of his passing with us. Thinking on those things, a smile began to creep across my face as I started to realize that Elijah's memory is being held in more hearts than I thought and that maybe God is still using his memory to draw people closer to Him. That's what happened tonight. I just didn't expect that person to be me.

Those T-shirts. Good Lord, how I am thankful for them. You read a little earlier how they've been used even more than in this instance. God has a flair for the dramatic, and I never grow tired of experiencing His goodness to me.

The trick in "experiencing" that goodness is to understand that my circumstances do not dictate His character. What I mean by that is that His goodness is always there, whether I feel or see it.

Wherever you are in life's journey, know that God's goodness is right there as well. You may be surrounded by everything that is not good. Don't let that keep you from seeing, very clearly, the God of all creation. If nothing else, know that this awesome God loves you. He always has, and He always will, whether you feel it or not.

Oct 17, 2014

I so wished today that I was still at Children's Hospital with Elijah. I know that sounds strange, but at least he would still be here. I know that is selfish, but if you have ever lost a child, you understand. I thought that the 6 weeks I spent in the hospital with him were the hardest because my mom was dying too, but that was just a test for what was to come. I just wished I had both of them for one more day. I just say all of this to tell everyone to LOVE your children, you never know what God has in store for you or your children.

Talk about being surprised! Paige wrote this, and as you'll read in my next post, that is rare and unusual. It seemed that God was pushing both of us to use our son's life and death to help others.

Oct 18, 2014

I never saw today coming. First, Paige surprised me by posting a status on here about Elijah and about how much she misses him and her mom. If you want to appreciate how rare that is, I'll tell you that I've seen her cry maybe twice over the past 6 years since they passed. She keeps her emotions to herself, and it's very uncommon for her to show, and especially write about, her feelings. So, you can imagine my surprise this morning as I read what she wrote yesterday. As if that little gift wasn't enough, I received another one today as we sat behind Paige's table at the Arbor Baptist Church arts and crafts sale. Most of you know that I can't resist holding a baby, so it's no surprise that I went looking for 9-month-old Samuel Ray not long after we had set her table up. He's the baby brother to Jonathan Ray, both of them sons to Mom and Dad's pastor, Keith Ray. Jonathan is the little boy who reminded me so much of Elijah when I first saw him, so this family already has a special place in my heart.

After finding little Sammy C (as I call him), he and I settled into a chair behind Paige's table to check out the shoppers as they came by. A few minutes later, he started getting sleepy, and almost without hesitation, I began to hum and then sing him the song, "Jesus Loves Me." The more I hummed and sang, the more he tried to help, and before I knew it, he was fast asleep on my chest, having sung himself to sleep with my help.

As I sat there listening to him breathe, feeling his soft blonde hair on my chin, I started thinking about what Paige had written. As a few tears welled in my eyes, I silently thanked God for the moment He was giving me. I thought of the many days that the little man on my chest was my own son and how I also longed for just one more day with him. I would sing that same song to him to help calm him or put him to sleep. It was that same song we sang to him on the Friday he took a turn for the worse, and the same one we sang at his funeral just days later. I thought of all the moments I had taken for granted when he was healthy and how the feelings I had on the worst days of his life were better for me than some on my best days now. But before I could start down that terrible road of sadness and grief, I was shaken awake by the words I had just sung. Do I believe those words, or was this just a nursery rhyme I was reciting to help a baby go to sleep? I was reminded that the journey of a Christian is not about ritual and recital but is a relationship that is very real. It has peaks and valleys, and

259

the same Jesus that I trust to save my soul is the same One I had to trust with my son. It may be hard, and I may get mad at Him, but His shoulders are big enough to take it. And guess what? He still loves me and gives me gifts like today...gifts that point me right back to Him and deepen the faith I claim as my own. Some days may be difficult, and I may long for just one more day with my son. But my faith reminds me that I have an eternity ahead of me with him, and more importantly, with Jesus...who loves us...this I know, for the Bible tells me so.

Little Sammy C blessed my heart that day as I appreciated yet another "glimpse" that God gave me. Our grief over our son was reaching its sixth anniversary, and we had found relief at the foot of the cross.

Grief comes in waves, and I didn't know then that we were between swells in this terrible ocean. I was about to start learning that we were in a lifelong battle, one that would require us to renew our minds and our hearts daily at the cross of Christ and one that would continue to test us as we tried to point others to the Jesus that brought us comfort.

Nov 24, 2014

My life changed 6 years ago this morning as Paige and I watched Elijah leave this life for eternity. In these past few years, I have concluded that there will never be a day when I do not think of him. I may live to be 100, but this hole in my heart will never fully heal, nor would I want it to. His memory will always be with me, and every year around late October, things are going to get hard, whether I like it or not. But that does not mean these times have to be the burden they can be. If I want, I can reflect on my son's life and see a lot more than the struggle that was so evident to everyone else. I can remember, if I choose to, the wonderful ways God showed Himself to me, my family, and to those around us. That is the one constant through all that we have been through—God's Grace. When I look to the past, I can see the fingerprints of the Hands that still carry us today, and the footsteps that I want to follow into the future. He is already there, bandaging up hurts not yet felt, forgiving transgressions not yet made. He has already prepared my days with joy through the trials and grief that will come even before I have ever opened my eyes to the morning. I have seen Him this last month or so as I have beat back the attacks on my mind that tell me Elijah's death was meaningless. He has used several friends to remind me of the truth and to help me remember God's faithfulness through those terrible yet wonderful days. So today, 6 years down the road, I will strive to continue the posture and position I assumed seconds after Elijah's death…on my knees, hands lifted up, thanking God for the life of my son.

It had been a difficult year for me, but that was made easier by friends who reminded me that my son's life was not wasted. Even with that, there was this constant feeling that my son's memory was fleeting and that he would be forgotten. The pain he endured; indeed, the pain I still felt was for naught if nothing or no one was changed.

It amazes me to think that grief is that powerful. It can tell lies that are easily believed, and in our weakest moments, we can fall for the most ridiculous of lies. It took a group of men around me to remind me that my son's life was still being used of God, if for no one else than myself. That should've been enough, but honestly, it depended on the day and where my walk with Jesus was.

Nov 6, 2015

Today would have been Elijah's 9th birthday. Say a prayer for us today if you care to, but don't ask anything of God; not today. If you want to talk to God on our behalf on this special day, I would ask that you say a prayer of thanksgiving. Thank Him for giving us our son, for the two wonderful years we had with him, for entrusting us with such a special gift, and for bringing us the joy he brought into our lives. Thank Him for walking with us through the good days, carrying us through the bad days, and for being faithful in the midst of our doubt and fear. Thank Him, as we do, for the lives changed, including our own, and for the laughter that can still be heard as well as the smile that will always be remembered. Thank Him for the fond memories that will always be held and for the day when we can hold him again. Thank Him for the beauty of life and death and for the promise of eternal life with Jesus. Finally, thank God for the life He has given you and for the loved ones who mean so much to you in your life. No one is promised tomorrow, and you never know when you might have to end your prayers as I silently do all of mine...Lord, please tell my son that I love him.

First off, yes. I still end any prayer that leaves my lips the same way. No, I don't say it out loud. It's a habit I started shortly after Elijah passed, and I see no reason to let it go. However, I don't want someone reading this to be confused, because Heaven to me isn't just my son. As a matter of fact—and we'll discuss this later on—Elijah will not be the first person I look to see when I cross from this life to the next. That honor is all for Jesus.

Let me go ahead and clear this up before we get to it in detail a little later. If someone you've lost and loved is what draws your imagination and fantasies of Heaven to fulfillment, you need to check yourself. Heaven is all about Jesus and seeing Him face to face. It's about being in His presence, and any desire we have that takes His place of honor is sin, plain and simple.

But make no mistake, I do look forward to seeing Elijah, my Grandpaw Partain, and others with who I want to reunite; that just can't be the primary desire of my heart. It can't be yours either, and if you're struggling with it, take that to Jesus. Ask Him to mend your heart to the point that He is the only desire you have. I'm not sure we can expect our burdens to be lifted until we a proper perspective of who Jesus is compared to who we are.

Nov 24, 2015

Today is the day that Elijah left us and this world behind for eternity and the glory of Heaven. He took his last breath and closed his mostly blind eyes this morning 7 years ago, and it started a season in our lives that has yet to pass. I can't put into words the pain that day generated, and I'm not sure you want me to try. But I will say this: Don't feel sorry for us. God has given us this road to travel, and it is not without His blessings. In fact, it is paved with promises we have come to trust, and within the guard rails of scripture, we find hope. No, promises and hope do not take away the pain and grief, but they do give those two God-given emotions some purpose in our lives. We do not hurt without the knowledge of healing, and we do not grieve adrift from the power of God's grace. Instead, we turn to our Savior for the comfort only He can give, and it is in the warmness of God's embrace that I know Elijah is whole, his blind eyes healed, his pain gone, and his laughter is heard once again as he experiences Glory with the same Jesus that is alive inside of his parents. His years are no longer numbered, and he is not constrained by the time that imprisons the rest of us. He is free, completely free, and he is in the presence of pure Love. I'm not sure I could ask for more, but I will from each of you; don't feel sorry for us… rejoice with us, because our son is in Heaven.

I think one of the worst feelings I've felt is pity from others. I really dislike people feeling sorry for us because our son died. This was the seventh anniversary of his death, and I wanted to convey to others that we're not to be pitied. God chose us to walk this road, just as He has chosen you to walk yours. Embrace it and understand that He knew every mile of it before you were born. That means that He sees every obstacle, every curve, and every pothole, and following Him will be the only path that truly fulfills you.

Dec 25, 2015

An empty stocking hangs on our mantle. We still put it out every year, even though it will never hold any candy or toys again. I remember when it held the little boy whose name is written in silver glitter across the front, and I can remember 2 years later as it sat boxed up with the rest of our decorations in the basement. We didn't feel like celebrating much that year. It just didn't seem right. But over the past 7 years, as the blinders of grief have fallen away to reveal God's promises to us and His plan for our lives, I have come to understand that the empty stocking represents so much more than what we thought we've lost. It represents life…eternal life. The Bible tells us in 2nd Corinthians 5:8 that "to be absent from the body is to be present with the Lord," and like every other word in the Bible, I believe it. So how can I be sad at the sight of this empty sock? Like death and the grief it brings, it may look like something to be pitied, but for the believer, it is so much more. It is a promise that we will forever be with the Jesus that saves us. I just didn't get it that first painful Christmas after he passed, but in the years since then, the truth has become increasingly clear. We aren't waiting on his stocking to be filled again; we're waiting on ours to be emptied. Once God's plan and purpose for our earthly lives are accomplished, we will be empty of the gift of time He has given us, and we will be called home to be with Him as Elijah has. So, the question is not what we do with the empty stocking on the end of the row but what we do with the other three that are full. That's my focus this Christmas morning: to be used of the One whose birth I celebrate and to honor Him with every moment He has given me. Sure, there's an empty stocking that hangs on our mantle, but I choose to live for the One who has filled the other three.

I think this may be my favorite post. Elijah's stocking still hangs on our mantle each year at Christmas. It's a reminder that we will always be the parents of two children and that his place in our lives is not forgotten. I look at it in the glow of the fire beneath it, and that empty stocking still fills my heart to this day. God could have given him to anyone, but he chose me to be his Daddy.

November 6, 2016

Today is Elijah's 10th birthday and our 8th time trying to figure out a way to celebrate it without him here. If there is a wish to be granted today, it would be for every one of you reading this, and not only for those of us who love him the most. I would hope that if you have children, you would understand the gift you have been given and the task you have undertaken. For far too long in Elijah's life, I did not. I took him for granted, that he would always be here, and that I would always have tomorrow with him. Then there was the day that tomorrow never came. Don't make that mistake. Love your children, celebrate with them, and hold them high. Be silly with them, and act like a fool, because the memories you're making might be all you have to hold on to one day. Make the necessary sacrifices to give them a better life, but don't sacrifice the time you have with them; that is what the best life is made of. And love them; tell them over and over again and show it every chance you get. Remember that you are showing them how to treat your grandchildren.

And before you start, don't feel sorry for us today. We're not living in a world of regret and sorrow. God has given us a hope that is more beautiful than words can describe, and He has bandaged up our hearts so that we can honestly say HAPPY birthday, Elijah, and mean it.

In the years since Elijah passed, I think that 2016 was the easiest year to focus on the truth. I walked through that October through November, praising God for my son. The lies of grief kept their distance, and I was able to focus my thoughts on all that was good in our lives. As we traveled through November that year, there wasn't any way I could feel anything but thankfulness for God's graciousness.

Nov 24, 2016

What are you thankful for today? That is the question that I opened my eyes to this morning as I consider what this day really means to my family. You see, this morning will mark 8 years since Elijah left us for Eternity and the glory of Heaven. Am I thankful for that? Some days I am. Other days...well, you can imagine. But if I've learned anything in the last 8 years since Elijah left us, it is how wonderful and fulfilling life can be if we choose to be thankful for what God has blessed us with. In the book of Ecclesiastes, Solomon reminds us to live in the moment and not dwell in the past or worry about the future. So, this morning, I think I'll hide those words in my heart, take a good look around me, and choose to be thankful for all of the blessings God has given...and even some He has allowed to be taken away. Happy Thanksgiving.

I'm not sure I can say anything else about this post. I was learning more each day and thankful to God for teaching me. But you know what comes at the end of a lesson, don't you? A test.

Feb 12, 2017

Still in awe of the little moments God orchestrates in our lives. A painful moment in church turned into prayerful worship when a new friend cared enough to notice that something wasn't quite right this morning. Instead of being imprisoned by thoughts of what never will be, I was reminded of the beauty seen only from the cover of God's hand. It's in the little things, folks, the small moments, where God does His most meaningful work.

It was children's day at church. As we celebrated the littlest amongst us, I felt the heaviness of the situation. After the song service, our new music minister asked what was wrong with me, so I told him the truth. To his credit, he didn't take a step back, apologize for asking, and say, "I'll pray for you." No, he embraced me, prayed for me, and came alongside me in that hard moment. Matt Fallin never met Elijah, but that didn't keep him from loving on his father. Like I said in the post, it's the little things. I think we see a lot of that in the life of Jesus. He paid attention to the little things.

April 27, 2017 ·

Sorry for the long post, but after talking with a friend this past weekend, I felt I needed to finally share this. These two pictures were taken almost exactly one year apart. The first is from Elijah's first birthday party, November 3, 2007. The next one was captured November 1, 2008, and in the past has only been shared with the closest of our friends. I am showing you these pictures because I want you to think about a question: Is God good? When looking at the first picture, the answer is obvious. Yes, of course, He is good. Elijah had miraculously made it through his first year of life; he had beaten the odds of being born 4 months early, made it through countless struggles and surgeries, and had finally made it home 5 months after being born. In short, he was a miracle, and only God could get the glory for the life celebrated in this image. You see Paige in the picture? She is happy, as we all were that day. Elijah is content in the lap of his mother, and all is well in our little world. God is, truly, good.

But then we focus our jubilant eyes on the next picture. Just a year later, we see the same two people in a very different setting; a hospital bed...again. Elijah is barely clinging to life, his body is weak, tired, and painful, and he is trying to find comfort in the only place he knows: the lap of his mother. Even though she is smiling, you can still see the dark circles of stress and worry under her eyes and the exhaustion that accompanies the last 2 months of staying in the hospital with him. Although it is only a few days before his birthday, there cannot be a real celebration. The only happiness of the day comes from some great friends who chose to brave the unseeable and love on us as their own family. Elijah is three weeks away from eternity, and even though this picture looks bad, it's not the worst one I could show you. Is God still good here? Through the pain? Through the worry? Through the worst of this life? It's not so easy to answer now, is it? What is the point of this? To help you understand that our God is much bigger than the situation we find ourselves in. He IS, by his very nature, good. Life still happens, often terrible, unspeakable things, to us and those we love. And sometimes God intervenes miraculously, but in others, He does not. His goodness is not defined by my personal experience or circumstances. His goodness is all too often missed in those moments when we have our heads turned looking for something or someone else. He promises in the book of Romans to work everything out for the GOOD of those that believe in Him, but often I get my good, and His good, confused. What that promise really means is that even in the most terrible this life can bring, He is there, working to ensure that in the most awful of days, His presence can still be felt. He is using the experience of life to show Himself to me. He may not change the situation, but He will use it to show you just how much He loves you. What you can't see in that second picture are the God-given friends and nurses who blessed us, the faith deepening challenge of walking with your child to the gates of Heaven, a church family that encircled us with love and grace, and the countless lives changed through the difficult life of a small child. So is God good? He was good enough to give us our son for 2 years, good enough to bring us through his passing, good enough to carry us through the worst of life and grief, good enough to deepen our faith, and is good enough to allow joy to settle where pain once lived. Yes, He is good, and should He allow my life to walk me down painful streets once again, I will still sing of the goodness of my God; He is good, and His love endures forever.

The two pictures I shared couldn't have been more opposite. The conversation I had made me realize that I needed to share more of my personal struggles with people. I needed to be real and let the chips fall where they may.

June 28, 2017

Today I have a class for work in Live Oak, Florida, so I stayed at a Holiday Inn Express last night. (No, that really doesn't make you smarter or more enlightened). As I checked in last night, the nice lady at the counter asked about the bracelet I wore on my right wrist when she checked my ID. I told her that my wife made it for me in memory of our son, Elijah, and that I wear it, or another like it, everywhere I go. After the usual awkward pause, she apologized for asking about it, and then said that she could never imagine how bad it must be to lose a child. Of course, this is nothing unusual for those of us unfortunate enough to have experienced this, but it reminds me of how impersonal people can be when facing these kinds of situations. It's not their fault, mind you; they simply don't know what to say when confronted firsthand with the worst this life can bring. I told her not to worry about it and then tried my best to explain that I actually love to talk about my son and that to share his story is to tell someone how great my God really is. That may not seem like the best answer to some people, but it doesn't make it any less true. How can you talk about the greatness of God in the face of your greatest fear? Again, it's hard to explain to those who haven't experienced it, but for those of us who have, it's refreshing to talk about the life of those we love. Don't miss that I said, "life."

You see, Paige and I will always have two children. It just so happens that one isn't with us any longer. That doesn't mean he is forgotten, that he never lived, or that we try to completely erase the impact of his short life on ours. What it does mean is that we are still proud to call him our son, eager to share how he touched the lives of other people, and ready to brag about him to any who would want to hear. So, the next time you come across someone scarred by the loss of a child, talk to them, listen to them, and don't let the awkwardness of the situation keep you from hearing the blessing of a life taken too soon.

November 6, 2017

Today would be Elijah's 11th birthday, and in his memory, I would like to share this picture/post with any of the Fathers out there who care to read it. This was the night of June 6th, 2008, and without writing my novel, I'll tell you that the next day was my D-day. Behind the smile I wear in this picture lived something of an uneasiness that was born as a twin with Elijah some 18 months before. What you're looking at is a father who is finally learning to accept his son...for who God had created him to be. The next day I would finally let go of the thought that there was something "wrong" with my son, but it was not before God had let me back myself into one of the darkest corners of my life. I had a tough time surrendering my dreams for Elijah and coming to terms with God's plan for him. My plan simply did not line up with God's, and I'm ashamed to say that it took me a long time to let go of my selfish will. By the time this picture was taken, God, in His wisdom, had allowed me to go as far as I could go.

The next morning, in the men's restroom of a suburban Atlanta mall, the battle to accept my son had reached the breaking point as I started to change Elijah's soiled diaper. At that moment, my heart was undone, and it finally broke free of the nasty prison my dreams and unfair expectations had created. My knees found the filthy floor of the crowded men's room, and as my hands reached for the God I cried out to, I repented and asked for forgiveness from both my God and my son. I was broken and ashamed of the father I had been. For all the fathers who may read this, learn from my mistakes. Don't waste any of the precious time you are given with your children by trying to make them fit the mold you have created. Love your children regardless of who they might be, and allow them to dream their own dreams while you support their efforts. Let God use them in their own unique way. I didn't want to accept that my son was blind and that he had special needs. It simply didn't fit into the narrative I had envisioned before he was born. God knew better, and the day after this picture was taken, I did too. His perceived disabilities no longer mattered; it was God's ability to use him that took center stage. What I learned to accept is that God had given Paige and me a blessing that no words of mine could ever fully explain. Although Elijah was blind, he helped others to see...even his own Daddy. His special needs never overshadowed his unique purpose, and it is only in retrospect that I see God's fingerprints throughout his short life. I almost missed it. Don't make that same mistake, men. Look at your kids through God-colored lenses and see the blessing that He has given. Don't miss the miracle and gift of life during the brief time that you have. Choose to encourage, to love, and to accept, while grounding your life and the dreams for your children in the truth found in God's word. In the end, that truth, expressed through love, will be all you have, and it is all that you can leave them after you're gone. Don't wait until it's too late. Don't wait until tomorrow to be the father they need today.

After posting this, the secret was out. My greatest failure as a father was out there, and I gave people permission to hold it against me. But you know what was also out there? God's grace, love, and forgiveness.

That's what I found on the floor of that men's room, and looking back, I can see that it changed me forever.

November 24, 2017

Nine years ago this morning, Elijah passed from this life into eternity. On most of the "anniversaries" of his life and death, my heart is heavy with the thoughts of what might have been but never will be. This morning is different; my heart is full as I think about Paige and what it means to have a godly wife and mother to my children. I know that without her, these difficult days would be unbearable at best and that our marriage would have been taxed beyond the breaking point as we struggled to come to terms with his short life and death.

I read shortly after Elijah's passing that almost 80% of marriages fail after the loss of a child. The reasons behind those failures are as different as the individuals who make up those statistics, and I'm not sure you could ever point to one specific cause. Over the past 9 years, I can safely say that without a woman the caliber of Paige, our marriage would have likely become another casualty of grief and loss, and we would have been part of that unfortunate 80%. Instead, the mutual grief we have experienced has drawn us closer together, and Paige deserves most of the earthly credit for it. Her quiet confidence and faith in God strengthen mine, and in the few times I have been allowed to see into her broken heart, I have seen a beautiful picture of Jesus unlike any before.

So, this morning, I choose to remember the love and dedication she showed our son throughout his life (especially during his last days), the courage she displayed in the face of our greatest fear, and the tenderness she has shown me through some of the hardest parts of this journey. Nine years of holding each other up, running to Jesus hand in hand, and choosing to refocus grief-laden thoughts into Christian service have helped to ensure that our marriage and commitment to God could not just survive but that it would continue to thrive, just as it did before. I couldn't make it without her; days like today would be insufferable, and my thoughts would drown me in a sea of sorrow and regret. This morning, however, my face wears the smile God used her love to create. Although I remember the life of our son, I am thankful for my wife, my companion, the best and greatest friend that I will ever have. Thank you, Paige, for walking with me through one more year, one more day, and one more moment, for choosing to live a life full of love, laughter, happiness, and joy regardless of the circumstances we may face together. Today isn't an anniversary of the end but is a reminder of the new beginning that awaits us. We will see him again, and I pray that when he and Jesus welcome us, they will have found us faithful to the last, still holding on to each other. I love you so very much.

Elijah's death isn't something that happened to each of us as individuals. We are one. We may grieve differently and in our own way, but we grieve together because we choose to. That's not a choice we made after Elijah passed. We chose each other when we were married by God in front of man. Yes, I wrote that correctly.

What I am saying is that when Paige and I recited our vows, we said at that time that we would take whatever life threw at us together. And you know what? Sometimes we have thrown things at each other. But in the end, we're together. What amazes me is how God equips us to minister to each other through our mutual grief. In the years that I have struggled, Paige has been strong. There are a few years where the opposite was true, and I can assure you that it was only by God's grace and miraculous power that I was able to speak truth into the heart of my wife.

March 15, 2018 ·

A long time coming, but I need to share this with a few anonymous people.

It's been almost 10 years since Elijah passed, and you'd think that the farther we travel down this road, the smoother it would be. Unfortunately, or maybe fortunately, that is not the case. Like the proverbial onion, there seems to be an infinite number of smelly layers to cut through as I continue to trust Jesus to deepen this faith that continues to struggle against such significant loss.

Over the past few months, as I've read my way through the book "A Different Kind of Happiness," I've begun to realize just how much Elijah's passing affected my relationships with other people. More specifically, it has begun to show me where I have failed to love well, and to make matters worse, those failures occurred between me and those who have loved my family and me like their own. In the years since his death, I have pushed friends away for superficial reasons and lashed out at others in anger, feeling justified because of the hurt I carried within. I have tried to hold people to standards I was unwilling to meet myself, and in the process, I have abandoned those who helped us through some of the worst days of my life.

What place does this admission have on social

media? What good may come, you ask? My hope is that others may learn from my shortcomings and that maybe some kind of apology, no matter how feeble, would kindle forgiveness that is not deserved. Loss, no matter how great, does not justify the judgment of others. In its deepest form, grief does not entitle someone to shut the doors of life and love on those who continue to knock with persistence.

To those I have pushed away, I am sorry. If I have shown anything other than the example and love of Jesus, please forgive me. I am still learning, still growing, still being refined through the fires of this life. I just never expected the flames to be this intense for so long.

This post was written solely for Jonathan and Christy Stuart. I didn't have to name names. Both of our families knew why it was written. Grief, and the anger often associated with it, will leave you as alone as you can feel if you give in to it. And that's exactly what I had done in the earlier years after the loss of Elijah.

Yet again, I wished to live part of my life over, just as I had done with the little time I had with Elijah. I guess what broke me down the most was this one thought: when will I ever let past failures teach me how to avoid future ones? I knew the answer was directly related to my relationship with Jesus, and I could see clearly the times that I had let the emotions of grief run wild in sin.

With that said, if you're reading this and you thought of someone you've hurt or have "written off" because of something that was said or done, I have a request to make of you. Forgive them. And then, forgive yourself as you ask them to forgive you. You'll be amazed at what will happen.

When I asked the Stuarts to forgive me, there was a freedom to rebuild the relationship we shared upon the foundation that was still there. Jonathan and Christy graciously forgave me, and today as I write this, there is a love between our families that is sweeter than ever. No, it's not the same as it used to be, but I'm not sure it's supposed to be.

Nov 7, 2019
Thankful for friends and family that remember when. Even if that "when" brings back memories too painful to put into words. You know who you are, and I can't thank each of you enough for bringing joy into our lives on days when that is in short supply.

I'm sure you notice the gap between those posts. I wrote nothing on Elijah's birthday or the anniversary of his death in 2018. There were two reasons for that. The first was that it was simply a bad year for me. Grief is like that. Some years are good, just as some days and moments are good. The year 2018 was not kind, and I used every bit of emotional energy I had battling back the lies and sadness.

The second reason is that I fell off a ladder the night before Thanksgiving. I broke my arm, hip, and pelvis. I was laid up in a hospital for a few days, and I didn't feel like writing. In all honesty, I was as broken physically as I was emotionally.

Nov 21, 2019
So today was the day. Eleven years ago this morning, I took a call from Paige that changed everything in our

lives. We knew it was coming but didn't know when. Unfortunately for us, it was this day; November 21st, 2008. What she told me, in a few short words, was that our son was dying, and although his body would last another three days, what made Elijah who he was, was gone. All that was left of him was a pale skeletal vessel that was weak and tired. After that call, it was simply a matter of time, and there was nothing any of us could do to change it. Why write about this? Why do I continue to reflect on a day that no one wants to remember? For the same reason, I have written about our son's life and death every year since he passed: to shake you and me out of the monotonous routine we may be in. Especially for me.

As a father, I too often get caught up in the day-to-day routine that makes sure we don't go broke and that we have enough to keep us somewhat happy. Happy...that's one way to put it, but in truth, anything and everything I do this time of year is a distraction from the grief that stalks and haunts me at every turn. Back to my point. What would you do if you received that kind of call today? What would be important to you if your child were three days away from eternity? How would you spend your time? What would you say to him or her that would echo through the halls of Heaven until you could join them once again? Trust me, you would long for that day long before it ever comes, and whatever words you mustered wouldn't be up to the task at hand. But here's my point. You don't have to wait. Speak volumes of love to your children and let them know just how much they mean to you. You don't want to know what it's like to talk to a granite stone in a field of tombs.... there's no response, at least not one that can be heard in this world. So, tonight, let your kids know that you love them, and that you're proud of them. Let them catch a glimpse of the joy they bring into your life every day, even if today wasn't the best day for it. You're not guaranteed another one, and you never know when that last "I love you" will be spoken. Leave them with the best you have to offer…with all that really lasts in this world: your love. That's what I sent my son to Heaven with 11 years ago….an "I love you" and the three of us singing his favorite song. For me, even that wasn't enough; it will never be enough. I thought I had a lifetime to tell him how much I loved him, and I did. I just didn't realize that the "lifetime" I had, was his.

I finally began to write again in 2019, and as I did, I saw that God was refocusing my thoughts and emotions. Instead of making sure people remembered my son, I was now trying to get other men to know their own. If you're struggling with grief, I would encourage you to use your pain to minister to and help others. You'll be amazed at how God will use your hurts to bring comfort, not only to others but also to yourself.

Jan 8, 2020

Are you ready for this day should it come? As a father? As a mother? Have you done all that you can to show your child that you love them? Not with material things that can be bought, but with a love that can persuade your heart to the evidence of that love when you stand where I do? Trust me. Things look and feel a whole lot different when your child's name is written on a granite stone. I don't want to bring you down from a social media page of "what if's" and "never will be," but I do want to encourage you to look at where your life, your sphere of influence, is in this new year of 2020. Forget about the gym membership, the "new you" that you need to show off to the world. Why not show your family the role model they really desire? Why not choose the new year to be a new you, and show your family what they really mean to you? No matter how physically fit I get, I will never be able to show my physical strength to my son, but the privilege I do have is to show my daughter and the rest of this world my Savior. I post this to remind you that this year may not be the year you think it may be. Things may not go your way. You may lose a spouse, a sibling, or, God forbid, a child. But know that God is with you. No matter how hard the circumstances, He is for you, and as my family learned in 2008, and every year since then, He will be with you. Don't take this year—this day—for granted. You never know when what you thought life would be will change. Choose to be what your family needs you to be today. You may not have tomorrow to set things straight, and this year's resolution may come a year too late.

This was written with an attached picture of Elijah's tombstone. I wanted whoever read it to think about where I was and what I was seeing.

When you're in a cemetery, at the foot of your son's grave, homework and chores no longer matter. The faults you see so clearly in your children fade. To be honest, there was a part of me that wanted to forget the times when I put my selfish desires for Elijah first and foremost, but to neglect that time in my life would be to take away the tools God was using to further mold me into a better father.

I can't go back and change it, but I can help other men change their present. If the pain Paige and I have been through brings just one parent closer to their child, it's been worth it. As a matter of fact, that one parent just might be me.

**

The next two chapters are somewhat out of place. I didn't initially write them for this book, but I also can't bring myself to leave them out. I wrote them as I studied God's word, unsure of why I was writing them. I'll share them with you, and hopefully, some of my thoughts will inspire you to go deeper into God's Word.

CHAPTER 18

ELIJAH IS LOOKING DOWN ON US...OR IS HE?

Hebrews 12:1-3 (NIV)
"Therefore, since we are surrounded by such
a great cloud of witnesses, let us throw off
everything that hinders and the sin that so easily
entangles. And let us run with perseverance the
race marked out for us, fixing our eyes on Jesus,
the pioneer and perfecter of faith. For the joy set
before him he endured the cross, scorning its
shame, and sat down at the right hand of the
throne of God. Consider him who endured such
opposition from sinners, so that you will not grow
weary and lose heart."

Let's be honest with each other. All of us have lost someone dear to us. Likely, somewhere amidst the gut-wrenching pain of grief, we have uttered these words, or something like them, *"I bet they're smiling down on us right now."* For some reason, we like to think that our loved ones who have passed on can still see us in this world. We like to imagine that we make them proud when we do something we think they'd admire. I'm guilty of it. For a good portion of my life, I have lived in the shadow of my Grandpaw Partain. I wanted to make him proud, win his approval, and I hoped he could see every good thing I did. The not-so-good? Well, I hope he had his head turned. Why do we never think about our loved ones seeing us in the midst of that sin we think we keep secret? Why is it that we only believe our loved ones see what we want them to? Does God turn their heads? Are they even watching us at all?

But I wonder if that is really what we want? Do we want this life to be more interesting than Heaven itself? Is Jesus that boring? I've been in church worship services where the preacher said we were witnessing Heaven on earth that very moment. I sure hope that wasn't the case. Emotions are a good thing, but they can get the best of us sometimes. For the record, I think it's a good thing to think about our loved ones watching us, especially if they left us a godly legacy to follow. That's what I believe Hebrews 12 is talking about. But let's not get too carried away with that line of thinking. Like all of scripture, we need to take into context what the writer of Hebrews is saying. To do that, we go back and read what was written before.

In chapter 11, the writer of this challenging letter walks us through the hall of faith, from creation to David and Samuel. All these great people were men and women of faith, but ordinary sinners, nonetheless. Then in chapter 12, the writer tells us that we are surrounded by this great cloud of witnesses, this righteous band of godly saints. But what is he really saying? Is Elijah looking at me? What about my grandfather, whom I admire and wish I could know so badly? Is he just a breath away, in some unseen dimension of reality that continues to walk this earth amongst us? I hope not. For his sake.

Don't hear me wrong; I think that thoughts like that are good, but with the proper perspective, with the clearest focus. I don't need to live my life with my eyes fixed on this world. I may live here, but scripture tells me that I am just passing through. My home is in Heaven with my Savior, with my son, and with my grandfather. And before I get lost in the thoughts of reuniting with those last two, I need to check myself. I should be all about Jesus…nothing else. My greatest desire for Heaven should be in seeing my Lord and Savior, face to face, in perfection, in person. I might remind us that He indeed does see all that we do on this earth, both good and bad. That thought sifts out another problem I have with my emotions in grief. Many times, my longings are not what they should be, and for that, I am ashamed.

Back to Hebrews 12. I think the writer is telling us that we need to follow the examples set before us. The word "witness" is exactly what it appears to be. It is describing someone with firsthand knowledge. In this case, we're talking about faith. The thought of those great people bearing witness to what I'm doing gets this whole idea backward. I should look back to what they have done, consider their great faith, and allow that to inspire me to know Jesus better. While that may be hard to do with the memory of my son, it is not impossible. The suffering that my son endured on this earth during his last days bears witness to the pain my Savior willingly took on for me. My son's blindness and special needs testify to the promise that God has made him whole.

And since my son now has sight, I'm not sure I want him to see his earthly father still trapped in this sinful flesh. Instead, I hope he is gazing upon the face of Jesus in worship of Him who has healed him perfectly and has bought his freedom from eternal suffering by His own. That's my prayer, my hope, and what I believe the writer of Hebrews is trying to get across to us. Look back to the lives of your loved ones and see Jesus.

If we continue in that chapter, we see what our response should be once we have our eyes fixed in the proper direction. A throwing off of hindrances and sin and running the race "marked out for us." In our context here, I think those words can mean a little something more than the first glance gives us. Let's take it backward so that we can gain a little clarity, shall we? "Marked out for us," tells us that God has a plan for our lives. Every moment has been laid out by His design. He sees all outcomes and has chosen a very unique path for each of us that results in the same wonderful reward if we are Christians; a closer relationship with Him. That's the prize, and that's why we must "fix our eyes on Jesus." If there is difficulty in my life, it is because that is the best way for me to see Jesus. It is by God's design.

But before we run, we must take off our tracksuit of "hindrances and sin." With grief and loss being our context, I might argue that fixing our eyes on anything except Jesus is part of that sin and hindrance. For me, thinking about what my son or grandfather *may* see pales in comparison to what Jesus *does* see. Are you getting the point? Am I? Am I living in the past, or am I pressing on in this race towards the ultimate prize?

You've never seen anyone win a race running backward, and you won't find a closer walk with Jesus by focusing solely on those who are no longer with you. That prize is only revealed when you focus on Who is always with you. Hopefully, by now, we all get my point. I hope that I will remember it before finishing the next paragraph, but then again, grief has ways of stealing our focus and attention.

Before I close this section, I want to encourage you. You may have read the last couple of paragraphs and thought that focusing on anything outside of the pain you have is all but impossible. The pain and hurt you feel are all too real, and it seems that no one can really understand what you're going through. Let me help you with this. They can't! We all handle grief differently. Where you are is where you are, and you, nor anyone else on this earth, can change that. Give yourself the gift of time. You need time to process whatever has happened in your life. The race the writer of Hebrews is talking about is a marathon, not a sprint. Run when you can, let Jesus carry you when you can't; but always, always, keep your focus on Him. Even if that results in anger, trust Him with the emotions you think are too raw and unfiltered. Remember that you are made in His image, and those emotions neither scare nor surprise Him. This was a lesson I learned the hard way and one that was gleaned from one of the oldest characters in the Bible: Job.

Chapter 19

WHY DID GOD ALLOW THIS? DOES HE CARE? WHERE IS HE?

Job 13:15a (NIV)
"Though he slay me, yet will I hope in him;"

A few years ago, our Sunday School class studied the book of Job. If you've never read it, you are missing out, and I encourage you to take a closer look. Like many life stories, Job's is one of mountain tops and valley floors as he struggled to come to terms with his view of who God is. We're likely all very familiar with phrases such as "the patience of Job," without ever really giving those words much more than a second thought. As I led our class through the poetic book, I tried to help each member find their common ground with our miserable character. Miserable? Yes. Throughout most of the book, Job is covered in ash, with painful sores all over his body, after losing most everything he loved and owned. He felt that God had abandoned him completely, and all his friends told him that he had done something to cause these catastrophes to come about. Even his wife suggested that he "curse God and die." In my mind, that might be the most misery Satan can stack on one human being this side of Hell.

Job may have been described as having patience, or perseverance as some translations read in the book of James, but he didn't obtain those qualities by keeping his mouth shut for very long. Job whined...a lot. I'm not criticizing the man because I've done my share of whining too. Like Job, I have felt abandoned by the One who is supposed to love me the most. I have felt that God simply did not care about my son's suffering and that He was not the All-Powerful God I *believed* Him to be. There's that word, *belief.* Let's save that for later. More to the point; God was not behaving like I thought He should in my life, and I struggled to understand how a loving God can allow someone's son to go through what I saw Elijah bear. It didn't line up with the fake smile and "God is Love" Sunday morning church mentality. But it didn't line up with anything else I have heard taught either. It wasn't until I let the Holy Spirit guide my heart through the book of Job that my view of God began to line up with the harsh struggles my family had been through.

I want to stop right here for a minute and take the time to make an even sharper point. Once again, I'll delve off into your life. Maybe you've been through something similar. Maybe you've experienced life events that leave little to no room for a loving God. Maybe you're looking for answers to why God allows the most terrible of things to happen to the most innocent. If so, then you're likely looking for answers that make sense out of the chaos. To that end, you probably won't find those answers here. What I write about is what I have found for my life, not yours. We are all on a very unique journey, and there is no "one size fits all" approach to healing and restoration. I am simply telling you how a faithful God worked in my humble life. If you dare to keep walking towards Him, He will provide you with the peace you so desperately need, just as He did for me. Peace and comfort are there, but they lay just beyond the horizon, on a path that is narrow and difficult. You will get there, but not before you travel the miserable road blazed by the likes of Job and so many others in scripture. The destination is worth the difficulty. You won't find what you're looking for anywhere else but at the feet of Jesus. That's where this unique road leads if you will continue down the path God has laid out. The specific course for each person may be different, but the destination is the same.

Back to Job. For the better part of 37 chapters, Job is in misery, and his friends have no answers to help him. Job is completely, and utterly, alone. Sound familiar? It certainly does to me. Grief has a way of isolating even the most social of people, and pain paves the smooth and comfortable road to withdraw into our emotions, closing the door on others and the outside world. A few months after Elijah passed, I noticed that I was drifting away from some of our closest friends, but I felt powerless to stop it. I'm sure Job felt that same way as his so-called friends were berating him day after day with their nonsense. Can you see Job? Can you picture him in your mind? Sore-ridden, ash-covered, with a shard of a pot in his hand; his nagging wife and unrelenting brethren casting their judgment on him. Have you felt as he did? Wait on chapter 38.

That's when God shows up.

God makes His presence known long before He speaks. An intense storm gathers, and a young man speaks what he thinks to be knowledge of the situation. The beginning of chapter 38 is like so many moments we have in our lives, especially if we're dealing with pain and grief. We know God is coming, but we're unsure when. And another storm? That's just what I need. I'm like Job in my grief. I want answers, and I want them right now. But when God finally does show up, He doesn't pull Job aside and answer Job's biggest question, "Why?" That alone ought to be enough to stop us in our tracks. If God doesn't give Job the why, should we expect it? That's what I feel like I'm entitled to when I operate in grief. I've been through this pain, and I deserve to know why. Or so I think. That's what Job thought, too. But God's answer is that He is God and Job is not. That's not especially comforting while you're sitting in the ash pile, but our location and circumstances don't make that statement any less true. We must leave God-sized things to God. In chapter 39, after God had questioned Job a while, Job clamped his hands over his mouth. I guess he had spoken enough. A little more of God speaking, and Job was finally able to muster up a few words in a meaningful response. What is Job's response to what God had told him? I love it.

Chapter 42: 3b-5 "Surely I spoke of things I did not understand, things too wonderful for me to know...My ears had heard of you, but now my eyes have seen you."

Job is saying that because of what he has been through, he knows God a little better than he did before, and he has "seen" God working despite his difficult circumstances. Wow! Until we begin to see God working like Paul describes in Romans, we will never get past the sorrow this world brings. If I can ever grasp that God will use everything in this life, the good, bad, and ugly, to show me that He loves me, I will begin to serve Him with a glad heart regardless of the circumstances in which I find myself; even when I have just buried my son. How many times have I seen God's miraculous work in my life, but unfortunately, it was only in retrospect? If you've seen nothing else in reading this book, I pray that you have seen the hand of God in the life my humble family has lived. The key, I think, is seeing the hand of God while you're in the storm, or as Job would say, "on the ash pile." That's my goal going forward without Elijah. I don't want to simply rest in what God has done in my past. I want to rest in the peace God offers now. Back to Job and his final chapter.

Job, like every Christian, was guaranteed a chapter 42 moment. If we will but trust the One who is leading us, we will experience it. God sees these moments even when we can't, and He is working to that end. I'm not talking about the material blessings Job received AFTER verse 5. I'm talking ABOUT verse 5. We are guaranteed to know God more if we will but press on through the worst, through the best, and everything else in between. The end goal of every Christian should be to know God more intimately, to draw closer to Him in relationship, and to trust Him with every aspect of our lives. That's the crossroads where I found myself during my struggle to accept Elijah's death, and I'm ashamed to say that it was years after Elijah passed that I finally realized the road I needed to take. Even now, almost ten years later, there are days I backtrack and take the smooth road that leads to doubt and fear. Once back at that crossroads, my faith is tested, and what I truly believe takes center stage.

***

In the second paragraph of this chapter, I mentioned the word belief, and I intentionally saved it for later. This is later. I am writing this over a decade after Elijah passed away. The events are still just as real, and the hurt is just as fresh. I doubt that will ever change, and I'm not sure I want it to. I mentioned earlier that Job's belief about who God is was challenged by his newfound circumstances. More specifically, how can a loving God, One who Job served almost perfectly, allow him to suffer? Heck, God invited Satan to strike Job; what does that say about Him? I try to rationalize my way through that piece of scripture and somehow make sense of the contrast between what I read and what I have experienced. I believe that God loves me, yet the hurt is still as fresh as ever. I believe that God loves my son, yet he suffered terribly. Like Job, I have a hard time seeing the bridge between the two. Where is this loving God when my life was being torn apart? I guess the answer depends on what I really believe about God. To find that out, I must look into the fire of the trial and see what is being rendered down. That will show me the kind of faith that I possess.

Do I believe that God loves both me and my son?

Of course, I do. Then what about the pain that I still feel today? Shouldn't that be healed up and better? Maybe a better question to ask would be this: Does that pain and anguish keep me running to Jesus? If the answer to the second question is yes, then I have my answer for the first. The Apostle Paul addresses this in 2 Corinthians 1:8-10.

> *"We do not want you to be uninformed, brothers and sisters, about the troubles we experienced in the province of Asia. We were under great pressure, far beyond our ability to endure, so that we despaired of life itself. Indeed, we felt we had received the sentence of death. But this happened that we might not rely on ourselves but on God, who raises the dead. He has delivered us from such a deadly peril, and he will deliver us again. On Him we have set our hope that he will continue to deliver us."*

Did you catch that? Paul knew that his suffering kept him from relying on himself. That goes against that old phrase, "God won't put on you more than you can bear," doesn't it? Pain and suffering kept Paul at the feet of Jesus, and it keeps me there today. So, what do I believe about God? I believe that He loves me enough to give me what's best for me, and that gift is a deeper walk with Him. He will give that to me at any cost to me or Him. It cost Him the cross and the life of Jesus. What is my little pain compared to that? Maybe it's time I embrace the cross, as He did, and die to self each and every day.

And what about my son? Why did he have to

suffer? Why must he die? That answer can't be to keep *me* at the feet of Jesus. The only world in which that answer makes sense is in one that revolves around me. I must ask that question *for* my son and not about him. Everyone has a date with death unless the Lord comes back first. That's life in this fallen world. But God could have spared Elijah; he could have lived a long, full life and died peacefully at the age of 92, surrounded by his family. Why didn't he? That's the question I'm really asking. What did God gain by taking my son at two years old? God didn't gain anything. Remember, God's design for us is perfection and eternal life. Man screwed that up. God is simply keeping up His end of the deal and dealing with our problems. I can't blame God for Elijah's sickness and still accept our place in eternity. In other words, God uses our messed-up world to show us His love for us. It's hypocrisy to accept that love, and then demand more, all the while sinning against the One we claim to serve.

That is a hard thought to get across, so I'll try it from another angle. Which is greater; to have Elijah never get sick, live until he's 92, and then pass peacefully in his sleep without pain or struggle? Or to take the cards life and this fallen world deal out, use them to bring good by providing for every need, every concern, and heal every part that is spiritually broken? The answer is clear to me, and I hope it is to you as well. No, God didn't choose to heal my son. He did something far greater and more impressive. He operates on a spiritual level that I can only catch glimpses of from time to time.

The last thought I'll share regarding Paul's writing is in verse 10.

*"He has delivered us from such a deadly peril,
and he will deliver us again. On Him we have set
our hope that he will continue to deliver us."*

There is no reason to think that just because I have been through one of the worst situations this life can bring that I can expect to never go through something just as terrible again. As a matter of fact, it was just four years later, in 2012, that I almost lost Paige. That story can be told later, but as with Elijah, over the course of a year, I watched Paige wither away into nothing. And you know what? God delivered again. He supplied every need in the midst of the chaos, and He came through time after time. Just as with Paul, with me, and with Job, He will continue to deliver you as well until, if you are His child, you are delivered to an eternity with Him. He sees every single one of your Job 42:5 moments, and He is already there waiting. Trust Him. Trust His perfect plan. He is the only one who will never let you down. He is the only one who offers the peace that surpasses the great loss I still feel.

THIS IS THE END

John 3:16 (NIV)
"For God so loved the world that he gave his one
and only Son, that whoever believes in him shall
not perish but have eternal life."

I knew at some point that this book would have to end, and I would have to start the long process of editing, checking, and rechecking every word and detail. Then, I must decide if I will choose to let anyone see it other than those closest to me. That thought scares me. I'm not sure I'm ready to place a bow on top of the gift Elijah's life was and is. So, in that mindset, I'll end this very incomplete work with this final paragraph.

If you have read this far, I want you to know one thing above all others; Jesus loves YOU. I have come to the realization that the reason my son loved to hear that song is that Jesus was singing it to me. I believe, looking back, that Elijah, though blind and mentally challenged, was used by God to remind me daily that I am loved despite how far I choose to run from Him or how slowly I turn to face Him. This prodigal father may always be stalked by grief and fear. Yes, I think I always will be, but if I turn around to fully embrace those two emotions, I must push Jesus and His waiting arms out of the way first. So, I want you to know, above all else, that you are loved more than anything, and you are cherished above everything, by a God who gave up all things, if for nothing else than for the privilege to pursue you as you run away from Him. Turn around. Turn around and see the beautiful face of Jesus.

ACKNOWLEDGMENTS

This book is dedicated first and foremost to the One who has given me this blessed story and life, Jesus Christ. He is ever-present and faithful through every moment. He is, as He promises in scripture to be, never-failing and good.

Second, this is for Paige, my beautiful wife. You love me and support me in ways I do not have the vocabulary to describe. Thank you for trusting me to write this story, our story. Loving you is the greatest honor and privilege I have been given, and you are, as always, the greatest blessing of my life outside of salvation. Let's keep proving them wrong.

For Maddie, I pray this book gives you an account of a time you cannot remember and shows you the depth of love you have always felt. Being chosen by God to be your Daddy changed my heart in ways I can't speak of. You are my "Busy," and I'm thankful that you have encouraged me to write out my brokenness. I pray that you see the face of Jesus clearly as you look at the life I live and the love I have for you.

To Brandi, thank you for being a guardian angel over our children. You'll never know how God used you to help this father's heart find a place of rest during the endless storms.

To the Stuart family, I can't thank you enough for loving my family and me like your own. Your friendship and unwavering support through the hardest of days mean more than you could ever know. Thank you for putting your lives on hold to minister to us.

To Dr. Fekete, thank you for walking with us through the hard times and rejoicing with us in the good ones. You treated our children like your own, and we could not have asked for a better pediatrician. Also, thank you for the cinnamon rolls.

To our church family and friends, this is as much your story as it is ours. Thank you for loving us with the love of Christ.

1 Peter 4:8-10 (NIV): "Above all, love each other deeply, because love covers over a multitude of sins. Offer hospitality to one another without grumbling. Each of you should use whatever gift you have received to serve others, as faithful stewards of God's grace in its various forms."

To my brother, Jeff, my pal. Thank you for being the one who listens without judgment and allows me the freedom to say the hard things out loud. There's no way this story looks like it does without you. You're the best brother anyone could ever have.

Lastly, but certainly in no way least, to my parents, thank you for choosing to anchor our family to the firm foundation of Jesus. I would not be who I am, nor would this story be what it is, without the beginning your love gave me.